KT-219-347

CONTENTS

LIST OF LINE ILLUSTRATIONS

The scenic illustrations are taken from drawings by
Frank Patterson.

LIST OF PLATES

INTRODUCTION

The *Britain by Bike* TV series was based on a collection of old and largely forgotten cycling guides written by Harold Briercliffe over 60 years ago in the late 1940s. Such was the interest in the TV series and associated book that the guides quickly went from almost unknown on the second-hand market to being highly prized and almost impossible to obtain. Perhaps the main reason for the renewed interest in the guides is that they take you back to a time many now see as cycling's golden era. They are so much more than slightly dated books with directions to help you find your way from A to B. Indeed anyone who sought out the original *Southern England* guide in the belief that it would provide accurate and reliable information about the best cycle routes around Southern England will be rather disappointed. Clearly, as a 21st century cycling guide, Harold Briercliffe's writings are no longer as helpful as they once were as so many aspects that impact upon cycling conditions have changed dramatically since the 1940s. For this reason, in this revised reissue the end of each chapter includes details of current recommended Sustrans routes that can be used to help explore the places that Briercliffe visited on his cycle journeys. The real joy of Harold's original books is their insight into Britain in an earlier age, and a reminder of a gentler pace of life and the attractions of cycle touring around Britain.

The starting point for understanding and appreciating the guides is to look at the context in which they were written. In the post-war years, Harold Briercliffe was a writer for *Cycling* magazine, then the UK's main cycling publication. The guides were assembled from the feature articles written in the magazine, with each issue covering an area of the UK that later formed the basis of a chapter within the regional guides. The first guide was published in 1947 and covered the Northern England region. Over the next few years a further five were produced ending with the Southern England guide, which was published in 1950.

The post-war Britain that Briercliffe encountered on his cycling journeys was a place in the midst of austerity, where rationing strictly controlled the availability of essentials, including food, clothes and fuel. It is worth remembering that at the end of the 1940s only 1 in 7 households had access to a car. If you were one of the few that did have a car your family's vehicle was likely to have little in common with today's air-conditioned people carriers and 4 x 4s. The most popular cars of the day were rather uncomfortable and modestly sized by modern standards with the Morris Minor and the Austin A30 being two of the most popular 1950s models. For most people, the main methods of mechanised transportation were rail, bus and, of course, the bicycle. With the average workers' holiday being only one or two weeks a year, the bicycle was seen as a key form of transport, offering cheap and easy access to the UK's places of interest (alongside bus and rail travel). During this period, the UK's cycling industry output was moving towards its peak. There were numerous manufacturers producing bicycles not only for the domestic market but for export all over the world. Notable companies from that era include Phillips, Dawes, BSA, Holdsworth, Royal Enfield, Elswick, Sunbeam, Evans, Claud Butler, Bates and Hetchins. But it was Raleigh that became established as the leading bicycle manufacturer of the day with the company's bicycle production reaching a peak of over a million in 1951. This increase in demand and supply was accompanied by advances in design so that bicycles became much more suited to longer distance touring. The use of lightweight 531 tubing to build the classic diamond-shaped frame (including randonneur handlebars), and the introduction of the simplex derailleur gear system and cantilever brakes, meant that the bicycles available in the early 1950s looked remarkably like modern touring bikes (although today's bicycles benefit from more sophisticated alloys of steel and aluminium as well as a much greater range of gears).

For those who might have been slightly less enthusiastic about spending their leisure time on a bike, there was relatively little to encourage them to stay indoors. This was a world without games consoles, personal stereos, home computers or wide-screen TVs. By the beginning of the 1950s only 8% of households in the UK had a TV. For the few television owners, there was only one station (ITV did not join the BBC until 1955) and the broadcasting hours were very limited. So for the vast majority, the radio "wireless" provided the main source of family entertainment within the home. Cinema was the only other boom area for entertainment.

Against this background of ongoing rationing and limited forms of entertainment, it is perhaps easier to understand the reasons why Harold Briercliffe (approaching 40) embarked on the monumental task of covering the whole of the UK by bike. Following production of the *Northern England* guide in 1947, Briercliffe's articles in *Cycling* magazine were gradually used to form a series of regional guides covering the Scottish Highlands, Wales, South West England, and The Midlands before finishing with Southern England.

The *Southern England* guide covered what Briercliffe described as a triangular area within the corner points provided by Banbury to the north, Margate to the southeast and Poole to the southwest. This area of Britain has experienced perhaps the greatest changes over the last 60 years, particularly in terms of housing and traffic growth. As far as traffic conditions are concerned it is revealing to see Briercliffe suggest the use of what are now very busy 'A' roads to cycle out of main urban areas. In the case of the *Southern England* guide the most obvious example of this is Briercliffe's suggestion to use the A4 Great West Road to cycle to Reading or starting from London Bridge to get to Kent, and Hyde Park Corner to head off to Sussex. His description of these routes does not refer to avoiding the M25 or the wider motorway network because in 1950 Britain's motorway network was still very much on the drawing board.

This gradual increase in Britain's highway capacity coincided with the growth in car ownership and use. The Department for Transport has recorded levels of use of the various types of transport (in annual billion vehicle kms) every year since 1949. Cycling has declined rapidly since the 1950s from a high of 24 billion vehicle kms in 1949 to around 5 billion vehicle kms in 2010. In the same 61-year period, car usage has risen from just over 20 billion vehicle kms in 1949 to almost 400 billion vehicle kms by 2010. Against this backdrop, it is little wonder that the road conditions Briercliffe describes at the end of the 1940s seem to bear so little relationship to what would be found if you tried cycle touring on Britain's trunk road network today.

In addition to this massive increase in highway capacity and traffic levels, Britain experienced significant house building in the post-war years leading to the expansion of major urban conurbations as well as some of our smaller towns and cities. There are many reminders of the obvious changes that have occurred since the 1940s in Briercliffe's description of the places he visits on his journeys. Briercliffe's route towards Reading involves passing through Bracknell, which he states "is likely to see great changes in the coming years". Great changes indeed! Bracknell was one of the 14 new towns designated by the Government in the New Towns Act of 1946. In the case of Bracknell its new-town status resulted in the transformation from what Briercliffe referred to as a small "townlet" (less than 5,000 inhabitants) to a major urban area with a population of over 60,000. The 1946 Act resulted in similar levels of development in a ring of New Towns around London, with places such as Stevenage, Crawley, Hemel Hempstead, Basildon and Harlow all growing rapidly. A second wave of new-town building followed in the 1960s, including towns such as Runcorn, Telford and Washington, with the grandest project being Milton Keynes, which was designated in January 1967.

You might wonder whether in the face of so much housing development, road building and traffic growth since 1950, if any of the UK that Briercliffe discovered on his journeys still exists. It is therefore reassuring to find that so much of the distinctive character of Briercliffe's Britain can still be discovered by the cycle tourist. An obvious starting point within the Southern England guide is to visit Oxford. The central area of this city has changed very little since the 1940s, and was left largely unscathed from World War II. So in the post-war years there was no need to undertake any significant rebuilding of the city centre. And due to the enlightened 'no road building' policies of the City and County Councils, there has been no need for significant demolition of old housing areas to make way for new roads. The benefit of all this is immediately apparent to the visiting cyclist travelling through the centre of the city. Today's cycle tourist will be surrounded by thousands of other people on their bikes in Oxford and will see a wonderful array of outstanding buildings including the Sheldonian Theatre, Bodleian Library,

Bridge of Sighs and the Radcliffe Camera. No doubt Briercliffe would still find Oxford "a most interesting and picturesque town".

Moving beyond the confines of Oxford, many of the routes that Briercliffe identifies in his journeys around the Thames Valley and the Cotswolds are still perfectly suitable for the keen touring cyclist. The network of roads and lanes around the Barringtons, Sherborne, Farmington and Northleach continue to provide ideal cycling country as do some of the roads linking villages in the Coln Valley. Towns such as Broadway, Chipping Camden, Chipping Norton and Stow remain wonderfully preserved examples of the best that the Cotswolds has to offer. And if Briercliffe was to return to Great Tew, his favourite Cotswold village, it is doubtful whether he would notice too many differences. But it is important to realise that some of the countryside routes suggested by Briercliffe have become so heavily trafficked that they are no longer suitable for leisure cycling. Examples include his suggested route from Enstone to Woodstock, using what has now become the A44 (an alternative Sustrans option, NCR 5, now exists). Similarly, the idea of using the A424 to cycle to Stow-on-the-Wold would perhaps be better avoided.

Moving beyond the Cotswolds and Thames Valley area, there are many other parts of Southern England where much of 1950s Britain still remains. The most notable example of this can probably be found on the Isle of Wight. Certainly Briercliffe is a big fan of the Island, commenting *"The tourist who wishes to choose a small neat region for exploration from a single centre could hardly do better, in southern England, than the delightful Isle of Wight."* The island has seen relatively little development in the last 60 years. As far as road building is concerned, most of the roads remain as they have been since the war and there is only one small stretch of dual carriageway on the island. There are currently over 200 miles of picturesque countryside and coastal cycle routes within a compact area of just 147 square miles. This explains why, in recent years, cycling has become a prime tourism feature on the Island to the extent that it now hosts an annual cycling festival.

Similarly, the New Forest has remained relatively unscathed by the passage of time since Briercliffe's visits in the 1940s. Places such as Lyndhurst, Brockenhurst and Lymington retain much of their old charm, albeit with increased traffic pressures. Interestingly, proposals for new road schemes within the Forest have not progressed. This passage of time seems insignificant in comparison to the lifespan of one the New Forest landmarks mentioned by Briercliffe. The Knightwood Oak remains a popular attraction today and is estimated to be over 500 years old, having been one of the Forest's well-known tourist magnets even in Victorian times.

One important feature that has changed in the New Forest, as elsewhere throughout Britain, is the availability of youth hostel accommodation. Briercliffe mentions the suitability of Norleywood Youth Hostel as a base for exploring the area. This hostel, along with many others mentioned throughout Briercliffe's guides, was one of the casualties of the hostel closure programme. This would not have been anticipated by Briercliffe back in the late 1940s when membership of the Youth Hostel Association was heading towards its peak. At the start of the 1950s there were 303 youth hostels and over 200,000 YHA members. Increased availability of holidays abroad and changes in the level of walking and hiking resulted in a gradual fall in demand for YHA accommodation. This led to closures and a modernisation programme with the emphasis on providing better youth-hostel facilities in towns and cities. The net result of this programme was that around 100 of the hostels (particularly those in more remote rural areas) were closed. So today's touring cyclists planning a holiday along the south coast will find the availability of YHA accommodation much diminished.

In terms of how to get to the south coast from the London area, Briercliffe's guide mentions a number of route options. He is particularly keen on the main route from Central London to Portsmouth, stating that the "*72 miles of the Portsmouth Road are perhaps the finest scenically of any main road between London and the South Coast.*" Users of the main road, now the busy A3, will realise that it no longer provides an ideal cycling environment. Instead, there are now a number of options for less busy routes developed by Sustrans, which are described at the end of chapters 4 and 5 (see pages 110 and 139). Many of the places Briercliffe mentions are still of great interest. For example, Guildford's High Street is described by Briercliffe as one of the most picturesque in the country. It remains a worthwhile stopping point with its "projecting clock" dating from 1682 outside the town hall. Also interesting to note is Briercliffe's reference to another well-known Guildford landmark: the construction of the modern cathedral building started in 1936 and by 1949 Briercliffe noted that it was well on the way to completion.

Leaving Guildford and looking at potential routes for getting to the south coast there is one option that was not available to Briercliffe. The infamous "Beeching Axe" which fell in the 1960s resulted in more than 4,000 miles of railway branch lines and 3,000 stations being closed. One unintended benefit from so many railway lines falling out of use was that in more recent years some of these routes have been converted to form excellent paths for cyclists and pedestrians. As cycle routes they have become a much-valued facility, free from the hazards of fast-moving motor vehicles and are generally very flat, not exceeding a gradient of more than 1 in 20. The network of available old railway paths can now be studied on the Sustrans mapping (see also page 141). One such path known as "The Downs Link Route" provides a 35-mile connection between Guildford and the south coast and is one of the longest converted railway path cycle routes in the country.

Moving on to the closing chapter of the Southern England guide, Briercliffe offers his ideas for a tour of the southern counties. What becomes increasingly apparent by this point is that much of the essential character of Southern England's towns has remained intact over the course of the last 60 years. It is noticeable that the routes between towns and cities seem to have changed more than the description of the towns themselves. In places such as Tunbridge Wells, Battle and Rye, much of the historic core remains. Chichester and Arundel still retain the wonderful buildings and architecture that Briercliffe mentions, including the Cathedral at Chichester and the castle at Arundel. You would however, no longer want to cycle between the two places via the A27. North of Arundel and the busy A27, the pleasant cycling that Briercliffe describes still exists in quintessential English villages such as Bury and Bignor. The towns along the south coast have, of course, been subject to much more development. For today's cyclist, travelling towards Kent new routes now exist (Sustrans NCR 2) to help cyclists visit the towns along the

English Channel, such as Eastbourne, Bexhill, Hastings, Winchelsea and Rye before heading on to Folkestone and Dover. Interestingly, back in 1947, Briercliffe makes reference to the exploratory shafts for the "often-proposed Channel Tunnel". It took almost another half a century for the commencement of the construction in earnest and for the tunnel to open finally for business. Who knows where Harold Briercliffe's journeys would have ended if there had been such an easy option for travelling in to France!

Mark Jarman
2012

PREFACE

THE scope of this guide to Southern England is a wide one. It takes in all the area—perhaps even a little more—that is enclosed within a triangle which has its apexes at Banbury, Margate and Poole. Thus it deals mostly with Londoners' country. Nevertheless, cyclists from the industrial Midlands and the North, living in a grimmer environment altogether than that south of the Warwickshire Avon, look upon "the South", as they call it, as one big garden.

Indeed, that part of the district which lies in Kent, Sussex and Hampshire, apart from a few blots, is singularly free from industrialism. Moreover, the weather is kinder for the greater part of the year than it is farther north.

The scenery of the district is pleasing rather than noble, soothing rather than inspiring. It has few hills higher than 900 feet, its coastline is nearly all spoilt by building and except for the Thames it has few impressive rivers.

Yet its own characteristics are striking enough. Throughout there are splendid examples of ecclesiastical, military and domestic building. There are great stretches of open moorland and down, plenty of woodlands and many pleasant, twisting, valleys.

Kent was for long the most advanced in the arts and sciences of all early English settlements and the power of the Kingdom of Wessex was so great that it extended far to the north—even into the confines of Midland Mercia, just as this guide to Southern England does.

The four main tours in this book cover, respectively:—

1. The Thames Valley and the Cotswolds;
2. Isle of Wight;
3. The New Forest; and
4. Kent, Surrey and Sussex.

There is necessarily some overlapping with two previous volumes in this series: South-west England and the Midlands. Where there appear to be omissions, the reader is directed to the appropriate companion volume.

HAROLD BRIERCLIFFE.

Letchworth, Herts.
December, 1949.

EVER READY

Cycle Lamps and Batteries

When cycling at night let Ever Ready be your guide. There is no more convenient and trouble-free form of cycle lighting than an Ever Ready Battery in an Ever Ready Lamp.

CHAPTER I

THE THAMES VALLEY AND THE COTSWOLDS

INTRODUCTION

IN the westerly and north-westerly directions, suburban London extends for 30 or 40 miles. Inside the arc Maidenhead—Berkhampstead there is a good deal of quiet and unspoilt scenery, but it is more worthy of the attention of the day rider or the week-ender rather than the man on a holiday. Beyond the 40-mile radius there lies a stretch of rural England which is lovely and varied and has very few marks of industrialism, if Reading and Swindon are avoided.

For a few miles above Reading goes perhaps the finest reach of the River Thames, and after a stretch of less attractive country comes Oxford. North and west of the university city undulate the Cotswolds consisting mostly of bare uplands, not greatly appealing in themselves but holding in their folds exquisite valleys and much splendid domestic architecture. This was all rich wool country in the Middle Ages and the stone houses and churches testify to its wealth and greatness.

The Cotswolds end at the imposing scarp which overlooks to the west the Severn Estuary, and in this vicinity are the richest woods of the district, at Cranham. On this western fringe, too, are some of the most charming of the deep valleys in the Cotswolds.

There are plenty of viewpoints in the Cotswolds, notably Cleeve Hill and Birdlip Hill (near Cheltenham), Fish Hill (above Broadway) and Edge Hill (between Banbury and Stratford-on-Avon). There is, too, a network of lanes, but an exception must be noted in the Thames Valley. It is not easy to follow the Thames closely by road, and glimpses of the river must be gained along the few reaches favoured with a riverside road or at selected viewpoints, mostly close to bridges and villages.

The district is, even now, fairly well supplied with bed and breakfast places. There are also plenty of youth hostels, although the inexperienced hosteller needs the usual warning that at week-ends hostels within 40 miles of the big cities are often uncomfortably full. Camping sites, especially in the remoter corners, are easily obtained.

Road surfaces, even on the minor highways, are quite good and once the Chilterns are pierced there are few of the flinty top-dressings which can damage so severely modern bicycle tyres with thin walls.

Nearly everyone who visits the Cotswolds comes home with a favourite village—the "most beautiful" is a typical superlative. I am as prejudiced as anyone else in this matter and I have my own ideas. Broadway is too sophisticated for me. Burford I would call a wonderful old townlet instead of a village. Perhaps I rate the highest of all, Great Tew (see page 40), which the purist might retort is not in the Cotswolds at all!

This leads me to the suggestion that there are quite a number of neglected places in the Thames Valley, Chilterns and Cotswolds. Fairford, for instance; Brill, on its hilltop; and Chipping Norton.

APPROACHES

The start and finish of this tour is at Reading, because that town is very accessible from London by road and railway and is also directly connected by rail with Bristol, Cardiff, Southampton and Portsmouth. The town can be reached readily also by rail from Birmingham, Sheffield and Leeds without entering London.

Tourists coming from the Midlands and the North, however, can join the route near Banbury, also an important railway centre.

The following tour is planned on the assumption of Friday evening rail assistance as far as Reading. The youth hostel and other accommodation north-west of Reading is always heavily taxed on summer Saturday evenings. Beds which may be booked up weeks in advance on Saturday nights can nearly always be secured for Friday—or any other week-day night.

The rider who elects to ride to Reading from London has, however, quite a pleasant prospect, especially if he decides to desert the main Bath Road, which does not become really attractive to the seasoned tourist until west of Reading. There are several useful routes in addition, however.

Those who must travel directly should leave Hyde Park Corner by Knightsbridge, passing along Kensington High Street to Hammersmith Broadway and then by Chiswick High Road to Turnham Green Church and the Great West Road.

This modern arterial road by-passes the congested streets of Brentford and Hounslow. About 11 miles from Hyde Park Corner, the Great West Road meets the Bath Road (A4). Here the way is rightward through suburbanized country past Cranford and along the Colnbrook by-pass to Slough, an old town now completely dominated by factories, and on to Maidenhead Bridge, where there is a first glimpse of the graciousness of the River Thames in the view northward to Boulters Lock.

Beyond Maidenhead, the course of A4 becomes more rural and the first considerable hills on the road are encountered. As the road draws closer to the Thames, however, the country grows tamer, except for a picture of the wooded slopes of the Chilterns in the north-west. There is another slight rise before Reading and then the town is reached past Palmer Park. By this route, Reading is 38½ miles from Hyde Park Corner.

Much more interesting, however, for the tourist with plenty of time are the two useful routes to north and south respectively, one mainly north of the direct road and the other to the south. They are slightly longer in distance and in time because of the wayside attractions.

The first continues along the Great West Road at Hounslow West and near East Bedfont joins the old road to Staines, first passing on the right Staines Reservoir.

There is not much to see in the town and the Thames is crossed on the way to Egham, beyond which the road cuts off the south-east corner of Windsor Great Park. Virginia Water, 21 miles from London, lies a little ahead and if the turn right beyond the bridge is taken, the south side of this artificial lake, 1½ miles long, can be followed at a short distance from the bank. This road, A329, is the way to Reading and it passes through a heathy district before coming to Ascot, with its racecourse on the right. Bracknell, the next townlet, is likely to see great changes in the coming years. A "New Town" is planned in the neighbourhood. A stretch of quieter country follows and then comes Wokingham, a pleasant market town, and thereafter it is a straight run into Reading.

The other road to Reading keeps closer to the Thames and is much longer and more picturesque than either of the two previous routes. It is identical with the main Reading road by Maidenhead as far as the first crossroads beyond the west end of the Colnbrook by-pass. Here the way is leftward into Datchet and so alongside the Thames before crossing Victoria Bridge and reaching Windsor by King Edward VII Avenue and past the Southern Region station.

Windsor, most famous for its castle, which has been the residence of the kings and queens of England for 800 years, is a "Royal" borough (the other is Kensington). The castle stands on a steep, low cliff above the river and dominates the district. Most days of the week (in the absence of the Court) the castle can be visited. To the south of Windsor lies Windsor Great Park, covering nearly 2,000 acres. There are several roads across this which are open to cyclists but barred to motors. The park was the scene of the Olympic Road Race in August, 1948, when the dismal weather did not prevent thousands of cyclists from witnessing the well-run event.

On the north side of Windsor Bridge lies Eton, consisting mainly of a long main street, with Eton College at its north end.

The route continues from Windsor along Oxford Road and Clewer Road, passing the racecourse in an eye of the river on the right. Farther along the Maidenhead road, down a turning to the right, stands Bray, famous for its vicar, who defied dislodgement at a time of religious strife. The by-road through Bray is recommended, thus missing the centre of Maidenhead.

On reaching the crossroads (the other road is A4, the main Reading highway) the way continues by going rightward towards Maidenhead bridge and then turning leftward and along the west bank of the Thames, reaching the pretty riverside village of Cookham. The view downstream from Cookham Bridge, across low land to Cookham Lock, has for a backcloth the woods of the Cliveden estate.

Bourne End, the next village upstream, is more commonplace, but Great Marlow is a pleasant spot where the river is crossed by a suspension bridge.

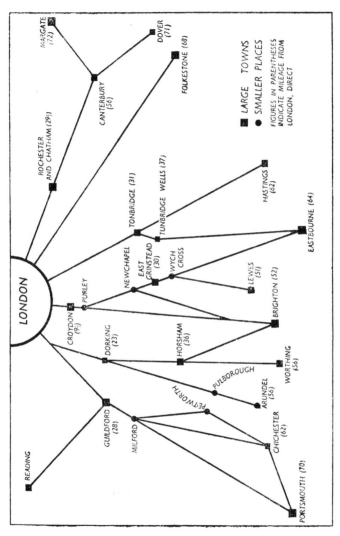

London to the Coast
(not to scale)

The next three miles of the route run south-west along the north-west side of the Thames, through wooded parks to a crossroads, where a left turn leads down into the well-situated riverside village of Medmenham. The main route continues pleasantly along the northern side of the river and then swings towards the south and into Henley-on-Thames.

Henley is the most sophisticated of all Thames-side towns. It is delightfully placed, however, and has a handsome bridge.

From Henley the route continues with A32 into Reading. Tourists using this approach from London can avoid Reading by taking a somewhat involved lane route westward from Henley by Greys Green, Cane End and Goring Heath to Pangbourne, on the tour described (see opposite).

Tourists travelling from the north and east who have reached Hatfield or St. Albans can make for Reading along the north and west side of London without entering the city or the inner suburbs. The route lies through Watford, Rickmansworth, and Denham, for Slough and Maidenhead.

Midland and Northern visitors will probably find that the handiest place to make for is Banbury, at the north end of the round. From Liverpool and Manchester, the place to head for first is Talke-o'-th'-Hill, in Staffordshire, whence the approach route passes through Newcastle-under-Lyme, Stone, Rugeley, Lichfield, Coleshill, Stonebridge, Kenilworth and Warwick.

This road to Banbury neatly skirts the worst of the Potteries and avoids completely Birmingham and Coventry.

From Newcastle, Yorkshire, Nottingham and Leicester, the best approach is probably through Doncaster, Ollerton, Nottingham, Leicester, Lutterworth, Rugby and Southam and so to Banbury.

Not far off this route there is a youth hostel at Badby (best approached by using a loop route from near Lutterworth, through Daventry and Badby), some three miles south-west of Daventry. This is most useful for those approaching from the north-east.

There is another hostel at North Newington, two miles south-west of Banbury, but this is hardly convenient for tourists following the route given. More useful is the hostel at Hanwell, three miles north of Banbury. This hostel is only half a mile east of the approach route from Liverpool and Manchester by Warwick. Hanwell is thus the most convenient hostel for those approaching Banbury from the north-west.

TOUR OF THE THAMES VALLEY AND THE COTSWOLDS
From Reading to Oxford—343 miles

Leave Reading by Oxford Road and go through a suburban district to near **Pangbourne** (5½ miles from Reading), a favourite riverside resort with a pretty annex across the bridge over the Thames at Whitchurch. On most week-nights it is possible to secure overnight accommodation here. On Saturdays, and the Sundays of Bank Holiday week-ends, most of the accommodation is booked well ahead by time trialists. Those who take a train to Reading on, say, a Friday evening, should be able to obtain a bed at Pangbourne, which thus provides alternative shelter to that at Streatley Hostel.

From Pangbourne the road keeps close to a lovely stretch of the Thames until it passes over the railway and reaches the village of Basildon, beyond which the river comes close again and there are excellent views to the meadows and gentle hills of the north-east hank.

Streatley (10) is a pretty village between the river and the steep hills to the west. The view from Streatley Hill is the chief natural feature of the neighbourhood. It commands the windings of many miles of the Thames. On the east bank of the river stands the pleasant boating resort of **Goring**. Streatley hostel lies on the west side of the main street, near the Bull Inn.

The way towards Oxford along A42 next runs past **Moulsford**, where there is a ferry to the quieter alternative road along the east bank, and into the small but historic town of **Wallingford** (16), with castle mounds and earthen ramparts.

From Wallingford tourists wishing to travel outward through Oxford—the return journey brings in the city—must continue along A42 through **Dorchester**—not to be confused with its Dorset namesake—now a small village, but formerly a Roman station and a leading Saxon town. In the 400 years before the Norman Conquest it was first a cathedral city of Wessex and then of Mercia. At the south end of the village, close to the River Thames stands the abbey church of St. Peter and St. Paul, a large building in Norman and Gothic styles. Leaving a bend of the Thames to the left, the main road traverses the woods of Nuneham Courtenay and enters Nuneham Courtenay village, a neat roadside place, and next runs by Sandford-on-Thames, Littlemore and past Cowley and Iffley, where the church is one of the best-preserved Norman structures in England. **Oxford** is entered over Magdalen Bridge and High Street, Details of the city appear on pages 43–44. Leave Carfax, the centre of the city, by Queen Street, New Road, Pacey's Bridge and Botley Road. Beyond Botley open country is traversed past Swinford Bridge, where the Thames is crossed, to the townlet of **Eynsham**. A little way ahead, the Oxford by-pass comes in from the right (this by-pass begins at Headington, on the main London-Oxford road, and stretches across farming country for 10 miles to the north of the city). Twelve miles from Oxford, the main road reaches **Witney** (see opposite). Wallingford to Witney, by this main road route, 25 miles.

————————

The recommended, quieter, route, goes north-west from Wallingford past Sotwell. On the right are the twin Sinodum Hills, also known as the **Wittenham Clumps**, because of the clusters of beech trees which top them, fine viewpoints in a flat countryside. The road descends to lower ground and past Appleford comes to **Sutton Courtenay**, a picturesque village standing on a backwater of the Thames, with old houses and many trees. To reach Abingdon, it is necessary to retrace a little to the east end of Sutton Courtenay and then to go across the river to Culham and left along A415 into **Abingdon** (31), an old agricultural town based on a formerly powerful Benedictine abbey, of which, a few fragments remain. Two old churches and Christ's Hospital, an alms house founded in 1553, and a seventeenth-century town hall are amongst the other "sights" of the town. Abingdon is a useful halting-place for lunch.

From Abingdon, the route then goes westward along A415 to Frilford, where right and then left, and on into **Kingston Bagpuize**, crossing vale country; next it turns northward and over the Thames at Newbridge before running through Standlake to Brighthampton and then into prettier country, partly close to the River Windrush, by Ducklington and so into **Witney** (46). There is no need for the hurried to enter the town at all—it can be skirted to the west.

An attractive alternative route between Abingdon and Witney goes first by the village of Wootton and then runs north-westward through lanes by Bessels Leigh to Eaton and the picturesque ferry at Bablock Hythe. Beyond the ferry is the historic village of **Stanton Harcourt**, with Pope's Study, the tower of a fifteenth-century manor house. To the west are the Devil's Quoits—standing stones. There are two roads into Witney, the usual route being by South Leigh, where Wesley preached his first sermon. This alternative route is unfrequented and is a trifle less in distance than the previous route.

Witney is on the River Windrush, a delightful tributary of the Thames. Witney blankets, for which the town is famous, are said to draw their freshness from the Windrush water used in bleaching and finishing them. Features of the town include a Blanket Hall and a Butter Cross, the latter dating from 1683. There are several places catering for tourists in Witney.

Witney should be left along the main Oxford-Cheltenham highway; which in 2½ miles reaches a point overlooking the Windrush and the old-fashioned village of **Minster Lovell**, seen on the right. It is worthwhile going down the lane into Minster Lovell. The grey houses, with their flat-stone or thatched roofs, form a pleasing picture. The church and the ruins of a manor house are to the right beyond the Swan Inn. A story attaches to the manor of a sealed-up room where the lord, hiding after a battle, was left by accident to die.

On regaining the main road, this should be followed past Charterville—the scene of collective farming experiments in the last century—to a hilltop (423 ft. above sea level). A lane turns right here into the valley again and to Asthall.

The main road goes straight ahead, keeping on the roof of the wolds, to Northleach. That is the way for anyone in a hurry, but there is much more to see by going down into Asthall and following the Windrush closely.

Asthall is a most harmonious Cotswolds village and is particularly well seen from the river bridge. The church and a many-gabled manor house are its chief features.

From Asthall the lane keeps to the south side of the Windrush and passes close to the scattered village of Swinbrook (on the opposite hillside) and also, on the far bank, the isolated church of Widford, which is well worth a call. The next mile or so the lane keeps close to the Windrush—and is liable to flooding—but soon the broad main street of Burford is entered at the foot of the hill which is the main physical feature of the village.

Burford (54) is one of the best-preserved old towns in England, and one of the most picturesque. Its situation on the side of a steep hill climbing southward from the Windrush is a fine one, as is the view looking uphill from near the Swan Inn past the pollarded trees. The town was of great importance in coaching days, but now the main east-west road passes it by. There is a variety of architectural styles about the houses and inns at Burford, but all are clearly of the Cotswolds. The church stands on low ground at the foot of the hill and close to the Windrush. It has a Norman west door and several fine chapels. Close by are almshouses, founded in 1457 by Richard, Earl of Warwick. Even the Methodist Chapel has a classical front. There are several inns and tea-houses in Burford catering for tourists. They are open on Sundays and all the year round—a point worth remembering.

North-east of Burford, and gained most readily by a lane leading from Swinbrook through Fordwells and Leafield, stands the picturesque fragment of the ancient **Forest of Wychwood**. Those with plenty of time should consider halting a night at Burford and making the Wychwood round by Leafield, Rangers Lodge, Charlbury, Finstock and Minster Lovell. The forest stands on high ground and there are many wide prospects. **Shipton-under-Wychwood**, four miles north of Burford and along the Chipping Norton road, has an old gatehouse which effectively disguises a cunningly adapted interior, now turned into a comfortable inn.

From Burford the recommended route keeps close to the Windrush, first crossing the bridge and then going leftward and reaching in 1½ miles the delightful village of **Taynton**, notable for its roofs, which are made of stone hewn at Taynton Quarries. These lie up a tributary valley of the Windrush in which the village stands. For some way the road undulates through pleasant meadows on the north side of the river and then comes **Great Barrington**, most noteworthy for Barrington Park which stretches to the west and is surrounded by a great wall.

The well-surfaced lane next dips down to the Windrush, where it is worth turning leftward and off the through route to see **Little Barrington**, where there is a simple church with a Norman door. These villages of the Windrush, quiet and old-world are amongst the most appealing things in the Cotswolds. The next place in the valley is **Windrush** village itself, a neat place where the course of the river turns out of its west-east direction and runs in from the north. The remainder of this valley journey lies up a tributary descending from the west.

Sherborne, the next village, has a picturesque row of Cotswold cottages. Beyond it the road passes the north side of Sherborne Park and keeps closer to the stream. The route becomes a field road, with gates, before it climbs into **Farmington**, where there is a Georgian mansion, a church, cottages and a number of large farms. From Farmington there follows a more exposed run into **Northleach** (65). The direct road between Burford and Northleach keeps to higher ground, is part of the busy Oxford-Cheltenham highway, and has little except its views to commend it. The distance is 9½ miles direct.

Northleach in the heyday of the Cotswolds industry was an important town. Now it is no more than a large village around a tree-bordered green. The church dominates, the Northleach scene and its magnificence has led it to be styled "The Cathedral of the Cotswolds." Northleach stands just east of the Fosse Way, the Roman road from Lincoln to Bath and makes a useful centre for the Cotswolds.

The objective of this part of the tour is Cirencester or, for hostellers, Duntisbourne Abbots. The direct route between the two towns runs along the Foss Way, and is 10 miles of open country—particularly hard going when the wind comes from the south-west. The hostel at Duntisbourne Abbots is gained by a cross-country lane route starting 7½ miles along the Cirencester road and leading by Perrotts Brook and Daglingworth. The hostel is actually six miles north-west of Cirencester. In bad weather or in any other difficult circumstances it might be best to make for Cirencester or the hostel directly from Northleach.

The recommended route, which will take over twice as long in time, brings in some of the most beautiful of Cotswolds valley scenery and several of the most attractive villages, and is altogether more desirable to the thorough tourist.

From Northleach the route first goes south-westward along the Fosse Way, the direct Cirencester road, for three miles to Foss Bridge. Just short of the bridge, a lane goes abruptly to the left and quickly enters **Coln St. Dennis**, first of the lovely villages which lie along the course of the River Coln. The valley is more beautiful and sheltered than that of the Windrush and there is more harmony about the eight villages which are to be found in the nine miles between Foss Bridge and Fairford.

Coln St. Dennis is particularly well placed near the river and its church tower rises from amongst green lawns. A long mile of easy going along the west bank of the Coln leads into **Coln Rogers**, where there is an old church, partly Saxon, amidst orchards in a secluded bend of the dale. For a brief stretch the road runs along the east side, and then turns a corner to enter **Winson**, aptly and alliteratively described as "winsome." Down the west bank of the Coln goes the road; the valley sides are steep in places and the turf is close-cropped.

Ablington comes next, a small village among old trees on the east side of the river. There is an old manor house close to the silvery trout stream.

The next of the Coln villages is the best-known of them all, **Bibury**, which stands on the Burford-Cirencester road where it crosses the river. The golden-brown stone of the Cotswolds has been wrought at Bibury into a manor house, a church and cottages, all of outstanding beauty. Most famous of Bibury's buildings is Arlington Row. The situation of the village beside the Coln gives the place a great deal of its charm and Arlington Row is finished off as a scene by the stream which runs in front of it.

From Bibury the hurrier can in seven miles of main road reach Cirencester to the west, passing through **Barnsley**, a pretty village with dormer-window cottages and gay gardens.

There is however, much more to be seen along the River Coln. From Bibury a more commonplace lane runs over high ground for 2½ miles to reach the riverside again at **Coln St. Aldwyn**. The village climbs up a hill between the mills and the church, from which the view southward is most charming, across lichened rooftops to the far hillside.

Beyond the bridge lies a crossroad, where a person anxious to reach Cirencester quickly could go right and in nine miles gain that town. However, there is still more to see along the Coln. For the painstaking, therefore, the way lies straight ahead and into **Quenington**, down a lane to the left. Once again there is an old church and many fine cottages and houses.

FAIRFORD.

Some 2½ miles south, reached by a road running alongside Fairford Park, lies **Fairford**, a townlet out of the hills and set amidst the meadows of the Upper Thames, although actually on its tributary, the Coln. At Fairford, the sight that tourists go to see is the windows in the church. These include portrayals of what is probably the liveliest set of devils in any English church. Satan himself is there. The more coveted place is shown, too, but it is the vivid depiction of Hell which lures the visitors.

Four miles east of Fairford lies Lechlade, a calm and restful place for a main-road town, with perhaps the loveliest church view on the Thames. Even here, so close to the source (see opposite) there is excellent boating on England's best-known river.

From Fairford, it is only nine miles of level going by Poulton and Ampney St. Peter into **Cirencester** (86). More information about Cirencester will be found on page 43.

The tourist is recommended to spend two nights in or near Cirencester, or at the youth hostel at Duntisbourne Abbots. Equally useful are bed-and-breakfast places at or near Bibury or Barnsley. The excursions in the following pages all start and finish at Cirencester, but the youth hosteller staying at Duntisbourne Abbots will find that he can link up with them quite easily.

The district north of Cirencester is varied and charming and deserving of a day of exploration. The outward route first leads north-westward along the Ermine Street, but a mile out of the town it turns rightward with A435 and continues northward up the Churn Valley. This is a typical bright dale of the Cotswolds, well wooded and with several pretty villages, the first of which, Baunton, is quickly reached and passed. At Perrotts Brook the hosteller can come in from Duntisbourne Abbots, some four miles north-west. The road continuing up the valley is a good one and, considering the hills around, is fairly level, rising imperceptibly for the most part. **North Cerney** is a pretty village with a restored cross. **Rendcomb** lies to the right but the road runs through its lovely park and for some distance its surroundings are very well wooded. At eight miles from Cirencester, where the main road turns towards the west, a lane bending rightward through the grounds of Colesbourne Park should be followed. This lane first climbs steeply through trees and then gains the walled upland before dropping into **Withington** (97), a village with a narrow street at a contracted part of the Coln Valley. Two miles south-east and reached by a hilly road past Cassey

Compton stands the remains of the Chedworth Roman Villa. This lies between the river and the Cirencester-Cheltenham railway and is reached down a lane running to the west of the road.

The remains can be seen on most week-days from 9 a.m. and on Sundays from 2 p.m. The villa is in the hands of the National Trust and includes a series of baths, a dining room and what are presumably dyeing tanks. The remains indicate that the site was once a busy one. They date from about the third century A.D. Nearby is a museum containing many of the finds discovered when the ruins were cleared. There is a small admission fee to the grounds.

From the villa a pleasant lane runs south-east by Yanworth to the main Northleach-Cirencester road at Fossebridge and then into Cirencester directly along this main road, A429. (Cirencester, second time, 109).

Cirencester lies a little too far east to serve as a first-class centre for the escarpments and woods of the south-west Cotswolds, and Duntisbourne Abbots, although closer to these attractions, partakes more of the valley and hill countryside of the central Cotswolds, than of the more vivid scenes of the south-west.

The tourist should therefore move his quarters a few miles nearer the Bristol Channel. This is best accomplished by taking the road westward from Cirencester, A4116, alongside the south side of Cirencester Park for two miles and then turning leftward by Tarlton. From this upland village a lane leads westward and into the charming village of **Cherrington**, well off the regular track of travellers, and at the head of a delightful valley. The interest quickens all the way down to **Avening** (119).

An alternative route between Cirencester and Avening lies through Tetbury and keeps to main roads entirely. The route runs close to the Tetbury branch railway line throughout and undulates a great deal. About three miles south-west of Cirencester is **Thames Head Bridge**, one of the reputed sources of the Thames. Two miles short of Tetbury stands the Trouble House Inn, associated with agrarian discontents of the past century. **Tetbury** (10 miles from Cirencester) has wide streets and an Elizabethan town hall on pillars in the middle of the town. The place is full of old buildings and is a useful halt for "elevenses". The Avening road (A434) runs northward, the last mile into the village being downhill (Cirencester to Avening, by Tetbury, 14).

From Avening the route leads pleasantly down a charming little dale. On the right the steep side of the valley climbs to **Minchinhampton**, well worth a visit for its breezy upland situation, old market hall, and the curious Holy Trinity Church.

The whole of this district flourished with the Cotswold wool trade. Now it is largely given over to farming but the old towns remain. Local stone is extensively used in domestic and farm buildings and the creamy-white of these, and the many stone walls, blend well with the grey-green upland meadows.

Nailsworth (122) typifies this characteristic of the south west Cotswolds. Here, the houses seem to be laid out everywhere amongst the hills, in tiers, clumps and apparent total disorder. Yet the ultimate effect appears most charming.

At Nailsworth, a sharp left turn should be taken, up a rise which carries the main Cheltenham-Bath road. After a rise of two miles, the hamlet of Tiltups End is reached. Here, to the west side of the road, lies the Tiltups End youth hostel. (124). There is other accommodation, for the non hosteller, in this neighbourhood. The hostel warden can advise. A stay of three nights is recommended in this neighbourhood.

The first day run recommended lies first along the main Bath road for four miles as far as the Boxwell crossroads. Here, the road going rightward and down into Boxwell should be used. Box trees on the surrounding hills gave the place its name. A little lower down the well-wooded valley, a right turn goes up into **Ozleworth**, which has a church with a tall hexagonal tower. Continuing west down the Boxwell valley, the tourist reaches Wortley, whence a pleasant hillfoot lane reaches the delightful small town of **Wotton-under-Edge** (135).

Wotton-under-Edge, despite its name, is placed on a spur of high ground and from its streets there are fine glimpses of the woods and green slopes to the east and north. The town is an old one and has a church with a lofty, pinnacled tower. The town is a good centre for an extended stay as an alternative to the Nailsworth and Tiltups End district.

From Wotton, an undulating foothills road, with fine views westward to the Severn Estuary, goes by North Nibley, leaving on the right a wooded hill on which stands a monument to Tyndale, who first translated the Bible into English, and under the finely shaped slopes of Stinchcombe Hill. The route then bends rightward, below Kingshill and then south-eastward into **Dursley** (141).

Dursley is a pleasing townlet, once famous for its cloth trade— and, much later, for the Dursley-Pedersen bicycle—and now like most of the towns in the Stroud neighbourhood making high-grade goods in a rural setting—and scarcely spoiling it. There is the accustomed market house on pillars and a graceful church.

Eastward from Dursley the route follows B4066 and gains the pleasantly-placed village of **Uley** (144). Even more secluded is the little retreat of **Owlpen**, situated down a lane which goes eastward. A sixteenth-century manor house is the gem of this retired hollow.

From Uley the route mounts sharply past Crawley to a long shoulder of hill and attains 807 ft. Just north-west of the road summit stands Uley Bury tumulus, one of the oldest prehistoric settlements in Britain and also commanding a most colourful panorama of the whole of the Severn Estuary between a point a little above Chepstow and Gloucester.

At a crossroads just north-east of the summit, a right turn should be taken. This leads very shortly to **Nympsfield**, which lies mostly to the north of the road. A little way southward the woods of Owlpen lie to the right of the road and there is a fascinating picture of **Owlpen** laid out below. At the next turning, the way lies leftward and eastward and so into **Horsley**, in a charming valley and so back to **Tiltups End** once more (150).

Another day in this delightful district might be spent in exploring the woods and valleys which lie to the north and east of Stroud. From Tiltups End it is an easy and pleasant run to Stroud, passing first through Painswick and then turning leftward to go northward down a picturesque valley by Woodchester and Rooksmoor and then over a hill and into Stroud (155½)

Stroud is one of the most interesting industrial towns in the whole of England. It is finely situated close to the meeting-place of five valleys and the houses rise on the broken hills in irregular terraces. Once Stroud was the most important cloth-making centre in the country. Today it still produces some of the finest of cloths. There are also engineering and other works, but the production is, in general, on such a small scale that the community spirit flourishes.

The way out of Stroud on this route is along King Street and B4010 in a north-easterly direction. This outlet keeps close to a stream as it traverses the charming Slad Valley. Beyond a snaky lake on the right, the route begins to climb to Bull Cross, from which there is a splendid view of Painswick (see opposite) on the opposite side of the valley. The road keeps to high ground, amongst heaths and woods, and gives peeps into graceful valleys to the left, notably above Shepscombe village which is revealed as a splash of grey buildings on a green hill.

Eight miles out of Stroud the road gains the summit of **Birdlip Hill**. Here the former main road to Gloucester drops down the slopes to the north-west at a gradient of one-in-five. The modern route runs north-east and descends to the Severn Valley by an easier drop past Little Witcombe. From Birdlip there is a fine view north-westward past Gloucester to the Forest of Dean and the Malvern Hills.

Birdlip is the farthest point to the north reached in this excursion. At the east end of the village, along the Cirencester road, a by-way turns rightward and in 1½ miles gains the small village of Brimpsfield. From it another lane runs southward, dipping into rich woods near Miserden and then climbing to the outskirts of Winstone. From this point the road south must be continued along a hill road which commands extensive views across a pastoral dale at the environs of Miserden and Edgeworth, both remotely situated to the west.

Sapperton (172) is a village on such a steep slope that the top of the church spire is lost below when approached from this side. From the village it is a sharp dip into the valley. Here is the western outlet of a 2½ mile long tunnel, now derelict, which formerly carried the Thames and Severn Canal to near Coates, on the Cirencester side of the range.

The Sapperton area can be reached also in short evening runs from Cirencester or Duntisbourne Abbots (see page 30).

———————

From Sapperton the route traverses the south side of the Golden Valley, a delightful run, to Frampton Mansell and then crosses to the north side by Chalford Station to Brimscombe, where a steep climb to the south leads over a breezy upland to Nailsworth and Tiltups End once again (181).

From Tiltups End, resuming the tour, the through route leads down past Nailsworth into Stroud a second time. Instead of going along the direct Birdlip road, however, the recommended route goes left and follows A46 and the Painswick road.

Painswick, which lies on a hill four miles north of Stroud, is one of the quaintest places in the Cotswolds. Its streets speak of antiquity and the fifteenth-century church, while beautiful in itself, is more renowned for the curiously clipped yews in the churchyard. South-west of Painswick, and reached by side roads, are Scotsquar Hill and Haresfield Hill, both of which command splendid views across the Severn Estuary.

From Painswick the main road climbs steadily past "Paradise", a farm name which occasioned one of the finest pieces of writing, "A Puncture in Paradise", by the late Fitzwater Wray, in "The Kuklos Papers."

From the summit, at 733 ft., the curving ridge of Painswick Hill strikes away to the left. Shortly there is a bewildering choice of by-lanes going left and right. To maintain height and keep amongst the glades of **Cranham Woods**, the finest in the Cotswolds, the third turning on the right should be followed—avoiding the lane to Cranham, also on the right—through grand woodlands to **Birdlip** (196) once more.

Here the direct Cheltenham road should be used. Nearly all the six miles into the resort are downhill. There are fine views across the Severn as the road descends Leckhampton Hill. On the right is The Devil's Chimney, a curious rock formation. **Cheltenham** is described fully on page 43.

Cheltenham must be left by way of Presbury Road, along A46. After two miles of level going, the road begins to rise sharply at

Southam, where there is a Tudor house, in timber, and stone, to the left of the road, and this steep rise continues for two miles during the ascent of **Cleeve Hill**. Just below the road summit, a right, turn leads to Cleeve Hill youth hostel (206) which is recommended for a stay of two nights. Non-hostellers should seek accommodation in the vicinity, either at Woodmancote or Bishops Cleeve (downhill to the West) or at Winchcombe, a charming small town to the north (see below).

From Cleeve Hill hostel there is some fine upland walking, across Cleeve Cloud and Cleeve Common, the highest point in the Cotswolds, 1070 ft. above sea level. From the hills and from the hostel there are far-reaching views across the Severn Valley and into Wales. The walk across Cleeve Common can be extended profitably by making for **Belas Knap**, a fine example of a Stone Age burial mound. A return might be made past Postlip Hall, a pleasant dwelling in a cosy nook and so to Cleeve Hill from the east. The lane running by Corndean Hall and Postlip Hall forms an alternative, daylight, approach to Cleeve Hill from the east. The surface is good as far as Postlip Hall, but thereafter it is but a farm road climbing steadily south of the main road to Cleeve Hill.

From Cleeve Hill, the main road, A46, descends in easy curves into the quaint townlet of **Winchcombe** (209½), where there are many old houses and inns, one of the latter, the "George" having a galleried yard. South-east of Winchcombe lies Sudeley Castle, while to the north-east and approached by a lane running southward off the main Broadway road are the remains of Hailes Abbey in a picturesque setting.

From Winchcombe A46 keeps to the foot of the hills with views of the Vale of Evesham to the left and the finely shaped western Cotswolds to the right. Just beyond the fork for Hailes Abbey, an alternative lane route is available by way of the picturesque stone villages of Stanway and Stanton. This alternative is recommended. It runs closer to the hills and is preferable, particularly at week-ends and holidays, when the main road is busy.

Eight miles from Winchcombe, the route enters **Broadway** (217½).

Broadway is a large, stone-built village, strung most pleasingly along both sides of the Oxford-Worcester road (A44). Its position on a main highway—on two main highways virtually—has given it a prominence which has not been altogether to the good. The prettiness and trimness seem to be overdone—and there is more than a little unnecessary artifice about it all: like a pretty woman who has made up rather too well. Remembering this, it is worthwhile to explore the village afoot; to see The Lygon Arms, dating from the sixteenth century; and to prowl amongst the old houses and to visit the old church.

Out of Broadway the main Oxford and London road mounts sharply for two miles up Fish Hill, which winds eastward up Broadway Hill to the Fish Inn at the summit. From this point there is a wide and chequered prospect north-westward across the Vale of Evesham to the Severn Valley and beyond. The view is even better from Broadway Beacon, a short way along a lane going southward. Here, at an altitude of 5,024 ft., there is a tower, built in 1798, and from it the eye ranges over a panorama as varied as it is beautiful. Beyond Bredon Hill, in the middle distance, rise the ridges of the Malvern Hills and in the north-west the hump of The Wrekin can sometimes be sighted. In spring, the vale below is fleecy with orchard blossoms.

The road, still A44, keeps most of its height for two miles, to the Cross Hands signpost, where the route leaves the main road and in three miles enters **Chipping Campden** (224½).

———————

An alternative route, for the explorer who is prepared to forsake the blandishments of Broadway for a by-lane route along the crests of the hills, can be started at Winchcombe. This route runs across lonely country, first going along the north side of Sudeley Park, to the east of Winchcombe, then climbing over Sudeley Hill (977 ft.) and undulating into a crossroads just west of the village of Ford there after running northward past Cutsdean. This village stands in a hollow to the east of the road and is worth a slight divergence to see its cottages and tithe barn. The route continues in a northerly direction and then gains Snowshlll, perhaps the most unspoilt and unassuming of all the villages in the Cotswolds—its position off the main routes ensures that. The route next turns to the north-east and in three miles from Snowshill reaches the Cross Hands, where the way into Chipping Campden lies straight ahead. This alternative route is about two miles longer than the one by Broadway.

Chipping Campden is probably the best-preserved of all the old towns in the Cotswolds. Its curving main street is a delight in stone; nothing seems out of place. The town lies off the main highways and can therefore retain its old-world air. Chipping Campden was founded largely during the fourteenth century, when the Cotswold wool trade was at its height. The market hall is a leading feature of the main street, while tucked away to the east of the town is a very fine Perpendicular church and some old almshouses. There are teahouses and inns in Chipping Campden for a lunch-time break.

At the south end of Chipping Campden a lane runs south eastward into **Broad Campden** (216), a tiny place, but pretty with stone wall and thatch, and then southward past the west side of Northwick Hall into **Blockley**, where there is a mill pond and a church, and so to **Bourton-on-the-Hill**, a village of gay gardens along A44.

From the village, the route still goes southward past Sezincote House and so to the main Broadway-Stow-on the-Wold road, A424, which should be followed southward into **Stow-on-the-Wold** (233½). There is a youth hostel here, at the east end of the square. The town has the reputation of being exposed to all the winds that blow and it is not surprising therefore that its buildings are found huddling closely together. There is bed-and-breakfast accommodation at Stow-on-the-Wold; it is a good centre and within reach of several of the most attractive of Cotswolds villages. An alternative halting place for the night is **Moreton-in-the-Marsh** 44 miles northward, a pleasant town of no great historical interest.

The tourist who has reached Stow-on-the-Wold could spend a summer's evening visiting some of the many charming villages within easy reach. A typical round of about 15 miles can bring in several of the loveliest places in the Cotswolds. The round leads first along B4077 north-westward for 1½ miles into **Upper Swell**.

Entering the village, there is a fine view of the trees and the water mill, the latter served by a lakelet to the north of the road. A mile south lies **Lower Swell**, a neat village alongside a pleasant brook. The church is passed first—it lies on a height to the east side of the road into the village.

Two miles farther south-west along a rural by-road the round reaches **Upper Slaughter**, a village built on the side of a hill. The manor house here is a place to note with its steeply-pitched roof. It is less than a mile south-east to **Lower Slaughter**, perhaps the most beautiful of this quartet of villages. A stream flows down the street between cottages and here and there are bridges across the water. At the east end is a church and a few larger houses.

Half a mile east of Lower Slaughter lies the Fosse Way. By going south-west along this, the railway is reached at **Bourton-on-the-Water**, one of the most engaging of the larger villages in the Cotswolds. A stream flows down the main street, through lawns, and is crossed by ornamental bridges. Behind the New Inn, at the south-east corner of the village stands a model of Bourton on a scale of one-tenth. This is an unusual and faithful reproduction.

From Bourton-on-the-Water a road runs south-east past the New Inn and then climbs eastward into Little Rissington. The place lines the lane and seems to be built into steps. A short way north stands the detached church of **Little Rissington**, where there is a notable view westward up the valley of the Windrush. The through road continues to climb eastward, gaining a ridge. Here the way lies leftward and then joins the Burford-Stow road, which is downhill as far as Stow Station, from which it mounts sharply into Stow-on-the-Wold (second time, 248½).

From Stow, the final stretch of the tour in the Cotswolds takes in the northern area, a bleaker district than even the Burford uplands and with two notable "sights" in the Rollright Stones and the village of Great Tew. From Stow the first few miles are mostly downhill as far as Adlestrop Station, whereafter the route climbs through woodlands to the open wolds at the Cross Hands public house. Here the way is straight ahead as far as a crossroads about 2½ miles past Cross Hands. At this point the way lies straight ahead for about half a mile, when, over a stone wall on the right, in a thin grove of trees, the **Rollright Stones** will be seen. These are in the form of a prehistoric circle. Close by are the Kings Stone and the Whispering Knights, other ancient landmarks.

The town of Chipping Norton to the south makes a fine cycling centre for the northern Cotswolds. It lies on a slope above a stream and is on or near several main roads. A few inns and other places catering for cyclists are in the town. The place is picturesque and well worth exploration afoot. In the north-west corner, rather obscurely situated, lies the parish church. More prominent in the market square are the classical town hall and the old Guildhall.

At a fork a little farther ahead, the route goes rightward, skirting on the right the scattered buildings of the isolated village of Great Rollright. Still lonelier country follows, as the route keeps to a ridge before descending into Swerford, which lies snugly in a valley. Beyond the village, the route climbs sharply past the farm called Potato Town and then reaches B4022, where the right turn should be taken. Beyond a drop to a streamlet and a rise, there is a left turn into the village of Great Tew (271).

Great Tew is one of the prettiest—if not the prettiest— of all the villages in the Cotswolds. Because it lies off the beaten track, it is not quoted as much as some places when discussion arises about the prettiest places in the district. The picture of the place is a complete one: every prominent dwelling has a thatched roof, there is no brick to mar the stone and the village inn is a host in itself. The stone has the warm, brown, appearance found in the north-east Cotswolds. To the east, in a graceful park, stands a stately hall.

From Great Tew, the line of B4022 should be gained. This road leads southwards, skirting Enstone on the east side, to meet A42, where the way is leftward to **Woodstock** (280), which stands at the gates of the park of Blenheim Palace. The grounds (but not the palace) are open on certain days of the week. Since the end of the war, some notable massed-start cycling races have been held in the grounds. The Palace, which can be seen from the park, was built to commemorate the services to the nation of the Duke of Marlborough and is in the Italian Renaissance style.

From Woodstock it is an easy run into Oxford, the final miles being through the northern suburbs. Further details of Oxford (288½) are on page 43. The youth hostel at Oxford lies over two miles east of the town, just off the London road.

———————

From Oxford, the main-road run back to London lies along A40, by Wheatley and Tetsworth and over the Chilterns by the picturesque roadside village of West Wycombe and the much less attractive town of High Wycombe and then past elevated Beaconsfield and along the suburbanised road past Denham and so into London (343). Oxford is directly served by railway from Paddington and the cyclist who does not care to follow the busy main road to London should remember the railway alternative.

———————

The rider who wishes to miss Oxford can travel from Great Tew or Chipping Norton over by-roads to the outskirts of London, passing through some quiet and attractive country. Another more direct route from the Chipping Norton district leaves A42 some four miles south-east of Chipping Norton and goes by Glympton and Bletchingdon to Islip and Stanton St. John, emerging on the Oxford-London road near Wheatley, some five miles on the London side of Oxford. This latter route is actually the fastest—and hilliest—route between Chipping Norton and London.

The quiet route from the north Cotswolds is much more attractive than either of these two roads. It is particularly useful on a busy day when the main roads are traffic-filled. From the eastern outskirts of Enstone it strikes eastward past the thatched cottages of Church Enstone and beyond Westcot Barton is a charming, rural highway through strings of villages. Just west of Heyford Station there is a pretty peep at the winding River Cherwell from an old bridge. Beyond Lower Heyford, the road (numbered B4030) runs through barer country, before running past the woods of Middleton Park and crossing the Oxford-Northampton road at Middleton Stoney. The next few miles into Bicester (18 miles from Chipping Norton) are more commonplace. **Bicester** is an old-fashioned town on the London-Banbury road and has catering places for the cyclist (Bicester is 55½ miles from London by the direct road through Aylesbury).

The recommended route follows the London road for 2½ miles,

but at the Blackthorn turning goes rightward, leaving Blackthorn village on the left as it bears towards the south with B4011. Across the levels to the south a prominent ridge rears up. This is Muswell Hill. Up the hill climbs a secondary road, which should be followed (the line of B4011 keeps to lower ground to the west). There are earthworks on the hill dating from the Civil War. Towards the south-east stands the village of **Brill** on a flat, solitary summit 694 ft. above sea level. There is a commanding view from the height. To the west the restored remains of Boarstall Tower are visible and beyond that the hummocky plain which leads to the upper Thames Valley and Oxford.

From Brill the route descends steeply towards the south-east, regaining B4011 and then proceeding along this highway into **Long Crendon**, a fascinating small town strung along the roadside and containing as its chief treasure a fourteenth century Court House, now owned by the National Trust. North-east of Long Crendon, on the banks of the River Thames, stand the remains of Notley Abbey which now form part of a farmhouse. (32).

From Long Crendon it is two miles into **Thame**, a small market town with a long rectangle of a square. At the south-east end of the town, the road breaks off and runs eastward into Princes Risborough where the London influence is felt again; then through lanes by Hampden Road and Hampden Bottom, taking in some of the finest corners of the Chilterns, and into Great Missenden for Amersham, Rickmansworth and the London suburbs. (Chipping Norton-London, by this route, 77 miles).

This tour, with halts at or near Streatley, Cirencester two nights), Painswick (three nights), Cleeve Hill (two nights), Stow-on-the-Wold, Oxford (or Thame), makes a good ten-day holiday which can be easily extended into a fortnight's trip by taking in the White Horse Hills from Streatley and/or the Edge Hill district from Stow-on-the-Wold, or Chipping Norton, as instanced on pages 44–49.

BRIEF GAZETEER

CIRENCESTER. E.C.D., Thurs. (Banbury, 39½; Bath, 34; Birmingham, 62; Bristol, 37; Burford, 17; Cheltenham, 16; Chipping Norton, 27½; Faringdon, 19; Gloucester, 17½; Oxford (direct), 36; Reading (direct) 53; Stratford-on-Avon, 40½; Stroud (direct), 12½; London, 88½).

A centrally-situated market town where several important roads, some of Roman origin, meet. There are scanty remains of the Roman wall. The great church dominates the centre of the town. It has a spire 162 ft. high and is mostly in the Perpendicular style. There is much interesting domestic architecture in Cirencester. To the west, lining the north side of the Stroud road, lies the vast expanse of Cirencester Park.

CHELTENHAM SPA. E.C.D., Wed. and Sat. (Banbury, 38; Bath 43; Birmingham, 46; Bristol, 43½; Broadway, 15½; Burford, 22½; Cardiff, 65; Cirencester, 16; Coventry, 50; Gloucester, 9; Hereford, 37; Oxford, 42; Reading, 69; Salisbury, 71; Stow-on-the-Wold, 18; Stratford-on-Avon, 30½; Stroud, 14; London, 95½).

A modern spa and residential town situated at the foot of the western escarpment of the Cotswolds. Hardly a resort for the cycle tourist, but a useful starting point for the foothills between Stroud and Chipping Campden and within easy reach of some of the most beautiful upland valleys in the Cotswold area.

OXFORD. M.D., Wed. E.C.D., Thurs. (Aylesbury, 23; Banbury, 23; Bath, 62; Bedford, 52; Birmingham, 63½; Broadway, 36; Buckingham, 24½; Burford, 20; Cambridge, 80; Cheltenham, 42; Chipping Norton, 19½; Cirencester (direct), 36; Coventry, 50; Derby, 90; Gloucester, 50½; Hereford, 79; High Wycombe, 26; Newbury, 27½; Reading (direct) 27; Salisbury, 60; Stamford, 77½; Stow-on-the-Wold, 28½; Stratford-on-Avon, 40; Warwick, 42½; Worcester, 57; London, 55).

One of the two principal university cities in England and a most interesting and picturesque town. The suburb of Cowley, to the south-east, is the location of the huge Cowley works of the Nuffield group of vehicle makers. The distant view of the city from any of the surrounding hills is a most pleasing one, largely because of the grouping of its towers and spires. The residential colleges are world-famous for their rich halls and chapels and for their green lawns. The most outstanding of the colleges are New, Merton, Christchurch, Magdalen and Oriel, mostly grouped close to the curving High Street which carries the main London road from the River Cherwell at Magdalen Bridge to Carfax, the ancient centre of the city, at the point where the east-west and north-south roads cross. Other notable buildings in the city are the cathedral, the Bodleian Library, the Sheldonian Theatre and St. Mary's Parish Church.

NEARBY TOURING DISTRICTS
The White Horse Hills

The distinctive, lonely region lying to the west of the Thames between Reading and Wallingford might be called The White Horse Hills. The northern boundary lies in the Vale of White Horse, which is threaded by the former G.W.R. main line to Swindon and Bath, and is now more famous for the atomic research station at Harwell, near Didcot. A convenient southern boundary is the Valley of the River Kennet, between Reading and Marlborough, through which the Bath road, A4, runs between Reading and Hungerford. Using Streatley (see page 42) as a base, the area could be explored hurriedly in a hard day of out-and-home riding. A preferable method is to stay a night at either Lambourn or Marlborough (where there is a youth hostel).

The district is composed mostly of open chalk downs, largely under the plough, although there is some delightful uncultivated country north-west and south-west of Marl borough and most conveniently visited from the town (see pages 45–46).

There is a direct, foothill route from Streatley to Wantage along A417 by Blewbury, but a more adventurous route is to go west sharply up the ridge of Streatley Hill (fine view) by Hungerford Green and through Aldworth to Compton and East Ilsley and West Ilsley and then by Farnborough and down a long slope off the back of the downs into **Wantage**, where there is an old church and a statue of King Alfred the Great, who is reputed to have been born here. The road west goes close to Kingston Lisle village. To the left of the road here, in a cottage garden, is the Blowing Stone, an isolated boulder with holes, which can be used as a fog horn!

Uffington, to the south, was the native place of judge Hughes, of *Tom Brown's Schooldays*. On White Horse Hill, to the left, where the downs are shaken out of their suavity into some shapeliness, can be seen the turf carving known as the White Horse. The route winds and undulates amongst the foothills and, through smaller places, gains **Bishopstone**, a very pretty village. A little ahead, the hill foot should be left for the mile-long climb to the Shepherd's Rest, or Totterdown Inn, where a lonely stretch (note the earthworks of Liddington Castle on the left) leads across upland to A345, near the village of **Chisledon**, a charming place celebrated for its associations with Richard Jefferies, the author. From this point A345 runs easily through a north-south valley through the downs by Ogbourne St. George, and into Marlborough.

More interesting to the inquisitive explorer is the lane which breaks away southward from Chisledon and then climbs The Ridgeway to Barbury Castle, a well-preserved earthwork said to be the scene of a fierce battle in AD. 556 in which the Britons were defeated. The hilltop, 879 ft. above sea level, commands wide views in all directions. From the castle, a rough upland route drops south-east into Marlborough.

Marlborough (London, direct, 73½ miles) is to the Bath Road what Stamford is to the Great North Road—an old town of marked architectural and historical interest. Stamford is the finer place of the two, but Marlborough has by far the richer surroundings. The High Street is wide and the shops and houses which line it are of varied styles, but there is no doubt about the dignity of the whole. There are churches to grace each end of the street. Gardens slope down to the side of the River Kennet. Marlborough had its heyday when it was a halt on the coaching road to Bath. It is nowadays as famous for its schools as for anything.

The youth hostel lies near the open-air swimming bath, while there is also other accommodation in the town.

Tourists with a few hours to spare could spend them profitably in the Marlborough area. Savernake Forest lies to the south-east; the Bath Road gives an impression of it in the last three miles into the town, but the thorough tourist who visits it from Marlborough should turn off to the right 1½ miles from the town along the Grand Avenue and explore the glades on either side. Oak and beech are the commonest trees in the forest, which is 16 miles in circumference.

Seven miles west of Marlborough, and reached along the Bath Road, is Avebury village, which stands in the Avebury Circle, the largest of its kind in England. There are a rampart and a ditch enclosing many stones, each about 40 ft. in circumference, and about 15ft. high. Towards the south-east runs an avenue of stones. Silbury Hill, which stands to the north of the Bath Road shortly before Avebury, is a mound with a plateau 130 ft. in diameter and over 100 ft. higher than the level of the surrounding fields. The circumference at the base is about 700 yards. The mound is computed to be a burial place of early historical times.

The DEVIL'S DEN
Dolmen on Marlborough Downs

North-west of Marlborough stretches a high and lonely land with few farms or cultivation. This area is famous for its sarsen stones, many of which can be seen from the rough trackways of the district. The Devil's Den lies on the downs north of Fyfield, three miles west of Marlborough on A4. It is a great cromlech, worth seeking out afoot.

Equally distinctive and remote is the country south-west of Marlborough. A steep escarpment, often rounded into graceful hummocks, overlooks the picturesque Vale of Pewsey. A short round journey past Dean and Walkers Hill, and so to Alton Priors and back over the downs again by Oare Hill would reveal the essentials of this attractive region.

Marlborough makes a good centre for a few days of quiet touring.

The whole of the upland around Marlborough forms the nearest truly open country to London, except for a few coastal stretches in Essex and Suffolk and parts of the North and South Downs.

From Marlborough the direct way to Reading or Streatley again leads directly eastward along the Bath Road through Froxfield to Hungerford, Newbury and Theale. There is much more to be seen, however, by the tourist who keeps north of A4.

The recommended route follows the road along the north side of the River Kennet, through **Mildenhall** (site of a Roman camp) and by Axford and so through the large village of Ramsbury to Knighton. The pleasant travelling down the valley is exchanged here for a lane which strikes north-eastward and northward over bare downs into **Lambourn**, an old and picturesque townlet set in the shallow Lambourn valley and amongst open country. There are opportunities here for bed-and-breakfast accommodation.

From Lambourn it is a delightful run down the valley through a succession of rural villages. The first, Eastbury, has a market cross testifying to its ancient importance; West Shefford has an old church approached by a lime-tree avenue; and the whole way is pleasantly varied and undulating into busy Newbury, on the Bath Road. From Newbury the road descends gradually along the Kennet Valley, past Thatcham and Woolhampton and so to a point short of Theale, where A340 turns leftward off the Reading and London road for Pangbourne and the highway up the south-west side of the Thames into Streatley (see page 23).

EDGE HILL

The tourist who has a day to spare when in Chipping Norton or its vicinity could spend the time very profitably by extending his Cotswolds round as far north as Edge Hill. This is a bold escarpment north-west of Banbury looking out across the Avon Valley: The hill marks the fringe of the oolite limestone belt from Dorset to Lincolnshire—the outpost of Wessex England and the scene of one of the earliest and least decisive of the battles in the Civil War.

From Chipping Norton, the first objective is Banbury, 13 miles north-east. **Banbury** (London, direct, 71 miles) is a market town, the centre of a busy district. The original cross was destroyed by the Puritans and the present "Banbury Cross" is less than 100 years old.

From Banbury the way to Edge Hill first follows the Warwick road going north-west and passes, on the right, the lane leading to **Hanwell** (see also page 23) which is a convenient halting-place for anyone visiting Edge Hill from London or Birmingham on a long week-end. At the road summit, some 5½ miles from Banbury, a lane strikes leftward just before the drop past compact and old-fashioned Warmington, on the right.

This lane (B4086) keeps to high ground, until it plunges towards Kineton, in the vale. A left fork, however, clings to the crest of the ridge and soon reaches, on the right, the viewpoint known as Edge Hill Tower. This was erected in 1750 and marks the spot where Charles I directed his forces. Kineton was the headquarters of the Parliamentarians and the battle took place in the fields between the hill and that small town. The Cavaliers were too hasty and lost the day because they deserted their superior point on the hill to fight in the Vale of the Red Horse. About 30,000 troops took part in the battle and over 1,000 were killed and lie buried amongst the meadows below the hill.

Just behind the tower, towards the south-east, stands the cul-de-sac village of Ratley, the prettiest in the district. Along the hill crest goes a lane which gives splendid glimpses across the valley. Briefly, the road A422—Banbury to Stratford-on-Avon—runs with the lip of the hill before plunging steeply down Sunrising Hill.

The route continues very pleasantly on the hilltop, through upland country broken by hedges and plantations. On the right is the site of the once-famous turf figure called the Red Horse, now scratched out of existence. About 4½ miles south west of the tower, the lane reaches a sheltered crossroads close to the "White House." Here a lane first rising sharply and going towards Whatcote village (north-west) should be followed for a mile to a point marked 611 ft.

above sea level on Bartholemew's maps. Down below, on the right, one of the most surprising and picturesque sights in England presents itself—the houses and grounds of **Compton Wynyates**. There are lawns and gardens and the 400-year-old house in Tudor style. It is generally possible to visit it on Wednesdays, Saturdays and Bank Holidays from 10-12 a.m. and 2-6 p.m. at a cost of 1s.

From the "White House" lanes lead generally southward by the villages of Sibford Gower and Sibford Ferris through Hook Norton and Great Rollright (see pages 39–40) to Over Norton and Chipping Norton once again.

This round of about 40 miles from and to Chipping Norton is mostly over unfrequented roads in a district which offers plenty of scenic variety.

Cycling in the Thames Valley
and Cotswolds today

As Harold Briercliffe wrote this cycle route guide in the late 1940s, many of the roads he mentions are now busier than they were and are not suitable for cycling today. Suggested alternative cycle routes, from Sustrans, which are in the same location as Harold's original route are listed below. To devise your own detailed route and map in the region, go to www.sustrans.org.uk/map for online mapping, and free iphone and android cycling apps.

The Thames Valley Cycle Route is part of **National Cycle Network Route 4**. The distance from **Putney Bridge** to **Reading** is roughly 60 miles. Highlights of this route include Hampton Court, Weybridge and the spectacular Windsor Great Park, which is part of the Windsor Castle Estate. The second part of this route is **National Route 5** from **Reading** to **Oxford** via **Didcot**, which includes the very picturesque Wallingford and Abingdon. This is 39 miles of minor road and traffic-free signed cycle route.

The Kennet and Avon (K&A) Canal is a continuation of National Route 4 from **Reading** to **Hungerford**. It is an almost entirely traffic-free route partly on the banks of the K&A canal, via **Thatcham** and **Newbury**. This is a 30-mile stretch of the K&A canal cycle route that roughly follows the canal all the way to **Bath**.

National Route 57 runs from **Oxford** to **Princes Risborough** and features the wonderful 7-mile disused railway path, the Phoenix Trail, between Thame and Princes Risborough. This route offers spectacular views over the Chiltern Hills and is dotted with interesting sculptures along the way.

Regional Route 47 from **Witney** to **Northleach** is a spectacular route known as the **Windrush Valley Cycle Route**. This 17-mile route will guide you past the National Trust's Sherbourne Estate and the picturesque market town **Burford**, which is well worth a stop.

Useful maps and books (available from www.sustransshop.co.uk): *Thames Valley Cycle Map; Severn and Thames Cycle Map;* and *Cotswold: Cycling Country Lanes.*

Currys are at your service EVERYWHERE!

Every ★ is a Currys branch

It's comforting to know, when you're touring, that you **are** never far from a Currys' branch. Each is *THE* CENTRE FOR *CYCLES* in the locality and **is** the one place where you can **be** sure of getting *any* accessory you want. In case of need, always HURRY TO CURRYS!

Currys LTD
THE CENTRE FOR CYCLES

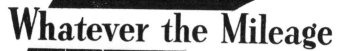
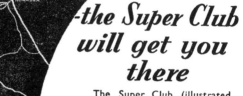

CHAPTER II

THE ISLE OF WIGHT

THE tourist who wishes to choose a small, neat region for exploration from a single centre could hardly better, in southern England, the delightful Isle of Wight. "The Island"—as its devotees always call it—is cultivated in both senses. By wise planning, a holiday of up to a week in length can be arranged in the Isle of Wight without re-traversing ground more than once or twice. There is certainly plenty to see on the island.

In the first place, the rhomboid off the south coast is a geological mix-up and that fact in itself ensures its variety. That mainland county of surprising geology called Dorset lends some of its surface rocks and clays to Wight. Hampshire has a hand in the make-up too. And then there is the sea, never more than a few miles away from any point on the island. The influence of the sea and a reputation for mildness and sunniness makes the Isle of Wight a favourite out-of-season touring ground for cyclists. Probably most wheelmen would prefer to go there in months other than July and August, when the catering places and the roads are likely to be too busy for the cycle tourist. Indeed, the weather of the island is so good that those who can should consider paying it a short visit in April or May or in October or November. Many London clubfolk are aware of this and the island has for long been a favourite Easter destination.

The best coastal scenery is to be found in the south of the island, notably west and east of Ventnor. Inland there are minor hill ranges and delightful folds in which old-world villages nestle snugly. There is quite a lot of woodland, too, and historic castles and houses, notably at Carisbrooke. At the extreme west end of Wight are the Needles and the picturesque sands of Alum Bay. The north side of the island is, in general, flatter and less interesting to the cyclist.

The clubman who does not mind steep hills and who seeks a centre which has a fine site, together with all the normal seaside attractions, would probably find that Ventnor makes the best seaside halt for a few days. Lovers of the remoter life should look for quarters in the interior of the island. There are youth hostels at Carisbrooke, Whitwell and Sandown, the two former being inland and the latter on the south-east coast. The camper should find no difficulty in securing sites at the farms inland or at one or other of the advertised and regulated camping grounds close to the coast.

On the whole, bed-and-breakfast charges are very little more on the Isle of Wight than they are on the mainland. Considering that it is largely a "pleasure island" and is in parts "fashionable," the Isle of Wight is reasonable enough in its rates—especially so out of the recognised holiday seasons.

The roads are now mostly good enough in surface. The cyclist should note, however, that the island has a network of 'bus routes and that the vehicles use, necessarily, the narrow, and winding roads. It is therefore desirable to exercise more than usual caution. The island's railway system is a delightful relic of another day, although quite adequate for its purpose, and efficiently run.

Novelty is the keynote of a cycling holiday in the Isle of Wight. Nowhere so near London can give such a changed atmosphere. The short journey across the Solent has a magical effect. Wight is another land, distinct, fascinating and, on acquaintance, lovable.

APPROACHES

The main approach to the Isle of Wight is from Portsmouth Harbour. There is an hourly service throughout most of the week and this is augmented to half-hourly at busy periods. The journey lasts 35 minutes and is interesting for its glimpses of naval and other shipping. There are pier dues to pay at the Ryde end. Portsmouth (see pages 89–91) is 70 miles from London (via Guildford), 50 from Bournemouth, 48 from Brighton, 80 from Reading, and 43½ from Salisbury.

Another approach is from Southampton to Cowes (Royal Pier), taking about an hour and at less frequent intervals than from Portsmouth. A further means of reaching the Island, particularly useful for those linking a visit with a tour of the New Forest, is from Lymington (see page 73) to Yarmouth. The service is at intervals of approximately 1½ hours during the busy parts of the day and takes 40 minutes.

THREE-DAY TOUR

(Three Day Excursions—from, and to, Ventnor
(or Whitwell)—96+ miles)

From Ryde, West Cowes and Yarmouth, there are roads converging on Ventnor or Whitwell. The usual route between Ryde and Ventnor goes through Brading, Sandown and Shanklin along A3055 . This is, however, one of the busiest roads on the island and between Shanklin and Ventnor has a steep rise and fall. The distance is 12½ miles.

A useful and quieter alternative is to turn right just beyond Brading and to follow the road by Alverstone Station and past Queen's Bower, a knoll with a good view, to Whiteley Bank, which is a 'bus junction in rural surroundings. The Ventnor road climbs steadily past the village of Wroxall and follows a little dale into hilly surroundings, amongst which the modern and unlovely suburb of Ventnor called Upper Ventnor is gained. Quite surprisingly, the sea appears ahead through a gap and then the tiers of houses called Ventnor. This route is only slightly longer than the Sandown approach.

From West Cowes, the road to Ventnor lies along A3020, past Parkhurst Prison and into Newport, the principal market town on the island, and then by Shide and Blackwater to Godshill. Ventnor can be reached either by Whiteley Bank or by the old-fashioned village of Whitwell (which has a youth hostel), from which the entry into the town lies along an exposed moorland road commanding splendid prospects out to sea and across Ventnor. West Cowes to Ventnor, 16½ miles.

The route across the island from Yarmouth is longer and more complicated. It runs by Mottistone, Brighstone, Shorwell and Chale Green to Chale, Niton (here hostellers bound for Whitwell go left) and Ventnor, a distance of 21½ miles.

Ventnor is probably the most sheltered of British seaside resorts. Its outlook towards the sea is almost southerly and it is therefore well protected from cold winds by the huge hill to the south called St. Boniface Down (787 ft. above sea level), on which the most prominent modern erections are radar masts, nowadays an ugly disfigurement. The resort was once almost exclusive, but nowadays it is a go-ahead place, with plenty of accommodation, shops, and cinemas. The pier has not yet been restored to its pre-war glory. Like many another, it was broken as an invasion precaution.

Most of Ventnor's buildings are in Isle of Wight stone and because there are very few sites for new buildings available in the town proper, it wears a late Victorian look, a dignified, even refined, appearance. In a word, it is a museum piece which has kept the atmosphere of the days of its creation and for that deserves preservation further. However, this splendour did not save Ventnor from the attentions of the Luftwaffe during the war.

Because of the precipitousness of its site, Ventnor is laid out in terraces and along these, going from west to east, or in reverse, the gradients are very slight indeed. Dropping down to the pier, however, from the station is quite an adventure. The gradients at the hairpins between one terrace and the one above or below are as steep as the turns are sharp and the utmost caution must be observed, as the roads are all narrow. A perpetual miracle of Ventnor is the ease and skill with which the 'bus drivers take the corners.

The main thoroughfare of Ventnor runs from the pretty Ventnor Park in the west, along Belgrave Road, Church Street, High Street and Trinity Road into Bonchurch in the east. Indeed, the tourist who arrives early in the day at Ventnor might well abandon his bicycle completely for an hour or two and explore afoot the coast and country to the east as far as Shanklin.

There is plenty to see all the way to Bonchurch, mostly of the cunning way in which road-makers and builders have contrived to secure a hold for their works. **Bonchurch** has far more foliage than Ventnor, of which it is now a suburb. A charming nook on the way to the old church is formed by a pond set to the left of the road and in sylvan, steep, surroundings.

The Old Church at Bonchurch lies to the right of where the main thoroughfare ends. It has a splendid site in a sequestered churchyard. The building is small and plain, but is beautified outside by roses and creepers.

A lane descends past the Old Church (which is left on the right) and soon becomes a well-trodden footpath above Monk's Bay. Soon the footpath (along which a bicycle might be taken, but not ridden) begins to climb into a jungle of small trees on a steep slope. There are tantalizing glimpses of the sea far below. On the right lies The Landslip, which last fell in 1818 and now forms an inland cliff.

The track reaches pastureland high above the sea and then dips to the head of **Luccombe Chine**. This valley lies to the right and can be explored as far as the sea. An alternative footpath, nearer the sea, can be used to return to Bonchurch.

From the head of Luccombe Chine the walk can be continued over high ground to a string of modern dwellings high above the sea. These are to the left of the road, but from a tea house amongst tall trees, to the right of the road, there is a glorious view across Sandown Bay, with Sandown laid out in the middle distance and the view bounded by Culver Cliff and the Yarborough Monument.

The descent into Shanklin is suburbanized but interesting—the traveller will be reminded by the varied building styles and the

SHANKLIN Chine

avenues of a vague similarity between this southern part of the Isle of Wight and the modern towns on the corniche routes of south-east France.

Shanklin is divided into three parts. There is the old part of the town, pretty with well-kept thatched roofs, in a hollow to the west; the new town, on higher ground which slopes northward towards Sandown; and, below the steep cliff on which the new town lies, the promenade and pier, both of which might easily be missed by the cyclist passing through Shanklin. The principal natural feature of the town is Shanklin Chine, a narrow crack in the greensand formation. Through the nick flows a streamlet and there is plenty of foliage above it. A small charge is made for admission.

The walk from Ventnor to Shanklin by Luccombe is about 4½ miles. There is a 'bus service for the return journey, which passes along the road described on page 65.

ROUND THE ISLAND

A strenuous day-ride of some 50 miles makes a memorable round of the island, starting by going westward from Ventnor and continuing in a clockwise direction. The first and last parts of the circuit are the hilliest. There are plenty of halting places for meals. The way out of Ventnor leads first along Belgrave Road and passes, on the left, Ventnor Park. Soon the road enters "The Undercliff", one of the most impressive natural features of the island and regarded as the most picturesque stretch of country on it.

The Undercliff is actually a series of natural terraces about six miles long and with a mean width of about 600 yards. On the right the land rises steeply in a cliff to the upland, while on the left there is a slope, generally less steep, leading down to the sea, which lies some 200 feet below. The landslip here must have occurred in early historical times and its cause was the moving of the upper strata of chalk and gravel over a slippery band of dark clay. The "slip" is now filled with a profusion of trees, bushes, grasses and flowers and this richness is the reason for the peculiar charm of this part of the south end of the island, usually called "The Back O' Wight". Holidaymakers at Ventnor can find some pleasant walks between the road and the sea. It should be stated that the course of the road between Ventnor and the village of Niton Undercliff is suburbanized. There are many detached houses, some in extensive grounds, with a few modern ones amongst them. The Undercliff, however, rises above this treatment and while it is not—could not be now—lonely and remote, it has its own charm and the final effect is one of foliage and seascapes rather than of Suburbia.

There are some large convalescent homes on the left soon after Ventnor, and after these the undulating road becomes a pleasing one, with stone walls and a great deal of woodland.

At a fork some two miles west of Ventnor, a lane can be taken off the route to the old church of St. Lawrence, at the foot of the inland cliff and with a view from the churchyard over the tumbled Undercliff and out to sea.

The next two miles are perhaps the finest along the Undercliff. The inland cliff rises boldly to the right and the ever-changing picture presented along the road keeps the eyes occupied.

Shortly, the country becomes less attractive. At a fork, the main route should be forsaken and the route past the Buddle Inn through Niton Undercliff taken. This was formerly the main coast road, but in comparatively recent times—in 1932—a serious landslip carried away the highway and when the road was re-made, it was taken higher on the hills and through Niton. This point was the scene of an earlier landslip in 1799.

Beyond the Buddle Inn—a sophisticated roadhouse nowadays—a lane runs towards the sea at **St. Catherine's Point**, but as this is private, the bicycle will have to be left at a house or hidden.

The outstanding feature of the landscape here is the lighthouse, a whitewashed building on the point. The light is a powerful one, familiar to all the coastwise shipping in the English Channel. Visits to the lighthouse can generally be arranged.

Just short of the lighthouse a field lane goes rightward to a farmhouse. To the right lifts the fallen cliff in a mass of hillocks, finally rising sharply at Gore Cliff into an imposing inland naze. A walker can pick his way across the landslip to South View House but the journey would be a toil with a bicycle as there is no regular path and the slithery blue mud becomes no more attractive on close acquaintance.

Back at the west end of Niton Undercliff, a short lane mounts steeply inland and passes through a gap in the downs before dropping into **Niton** village, a large village, where the way is leftward and upward along a new road across bare upland which commands from a level of some 400 ft. a remarkable panorama of the whole of the uniform southwest coast as far as The Needles. Leaving St. Catherine's Hill on the right, the road sweeps downward.

St. Catherine's Hill, 785 ft. above sea level and therefore almost the highest point in the Isle of Wight, is a viewpoint which embraces neatly the entire island. The view is extensive rather than memorable, the chalk cliffs at Highdown, west of Freshwater (towards the north west) being perhaps the strongest feature. The ruins on the hilltop are of two lighthouses, one dating from the Middle Ages and the other from the eighteenth century. The erection to the north end of the narrowing down is Hoy's Pillar, which has conflicting notices of its purpose, both of them concerned with nineteenth-century Russia.

Where the new road joins the old is **Blackgang Chine** one of the commercialised little dales running down to the sea. A touch of the bizarre is provided by the skeleton of the body of a whale which came ashore at Alum Bay 150 years ago.

It is worth continuing past the head of the chine along the former road to Niton Undercliff. The road ends abruptly beyond Southview House, from the vicinity of which is the finest view of this part of the coast. The land curves upward from the sea through the fallen landslip and over dense brushwood to the rugged and arresting summit of Gore Cliff and Windcliffe, which lies beyond. The tourist must return to Blackgang again because of the landslip.

The next village is **Chale** (seven miles from Ventnor, direct), a scattered place lying on the western slope of St. Catherine's Hill. There is a church with a Perpendicular tower at Chale, and just north of it, an inn where snacks are obtainable.

At Chale church commences the former "Military Road" to Freshwater Bay. This keeps to within about 400 yards of the low cliff edge and is lonely for most of the seven miles to Brook. The going is indifferent for much of the distance and the road cannot be recommended to those in a hurry. It is, however, useful for riders making a leisurely examination of the coastline and the many chines thereon. The finest of these chines is **Whale Chine**, about a mile north-west of Chale.

The through route goes inland by Chale Green and then across less interesting country to **Shorwell** (11½) which is delightfully situated in a dip in the chalk range. There is an interesting church in the village and as he leaves it, going west, the tourist should look to the left for West Court Manor House, a picturesque building.

From near this point there is a good view of the cliffs as far as Highdown. Another picturesque farmhouse can be seen at Limerstone a short way on. **Brighstone** (13½), a pleasant village,

lies under the sheltering, wooded range called Brighstone Down. **Mottistone** has a sixteenth-century manor house. Half a mile west is **Hulverstone,** where the main road goes rightward. The tourist will prefer to go leftward into **Brook**, a picturesque village near the sea. From it, a lane keeps close to the coast and has fine views of the Freshwater cliffs. The lane gradually mounts the side of Afton Down and soon reaches **Freshwater Bay** (21), nowadays a thriving resort. The whole of the western end of the island is popular and much of the land is built on. The cliffs of Highdown, to the west are National Trust property and accessible. Tourists with time to spare could walk to the summit of the down (485 ft.) a distance of about a mile.

From Freshwater Bay to Alum Bay and The Needles by road is about three miles in all. The route goes inland past Farringford House, once the home of Tennyson, and then passes over higher ground before dropping to **Alum Bay** (24).

Alum Bay is greatly frequented by holidaymakers, who visit it mostly from larger resorts, even those on the mainland. Its natural claim to fame lies in the coloured cliffs which stretch south-westward towards The Needles. The cliffs are an exposure of the complex geological structure of the Isle of Wight and are at their best after heavy rain.

The Needles lie farther out and can be approached on foot along the cliff edge above Alum Bay. They consist of detached rocks, on the outermost of which stands a lighthouse. To the south side of the headland are the white chalk cliffs of Scratchell's Bay and the Grand Arch, an aperture 200 ft. high, which is probably the finest natural arch in England.

From Alum Bay, the tourist should begin to travel north-east, passing on the landward side of imposing Headon Hill and then descending to the resort of **Totland Bay** (26), where the houses are raised above shore level, and inland to the broad mouth of the estuary of the River Yar, crossed by a long causeway and a bridge.

Yarmouth (29) is an old-fashioned townlet which has castle remains. It is more suitable as a lunch place for the cyclist than either Alum Bay or Totland Bay.

The next part of the route lies through country quite different from that encountered previously. By some standards it is quite dull, but as a cycling district it is very pleasant indeed, with low-lying country and without steep hills.

From Yarmouth the road to take is along High Street and for about half a mile along the edge of The Solent, from which stretch there are pleasing pictures across the water at the rising ground behind Lymington and at the flowing contours of the New Forest beyond.

Shalfleet, the first village, has a church tower which seems to have been built for defence. Beyond it the road rises to a fork, where the main thoroughfare lies straight ahead into Newport (see pages 66–67), the commercial capital of the island, some six miles east.

The recommended route bends leftward and north-eastward, however, and passes over creeks before gaining a left fork which leads down a cul-de-sac into **Newtown**. The short side journey off the main road is well worthwhile, for Newtown is one of the most remarkable examples in England of how the fortunes of places, as of men, ebb and flow.

The eighteenth century Town Hall is a symbol of Newtown's former importance. The place is now little more than a village standing on an isolated peninsula between two wide creeks. Salt manufactures and oyster cultivation helped to make it, but as long ago as the year 1001, the Danes came and burnt it down. In 1256, the town received a charters and in 2377 the French, too, carried out a raid. Some of the ancient streets of the town are nowadays nothing but lanes.

Gold Street leads eastward and back to the lane route towards Cowes. The route winds north-eastward, leaving on the right the woods of Parkhurst Forest, beyond which is Parkhurst Prison. The main way enters Cowes (41) from the south-west, but there is an alternative by the small coast resort of Gurnard Bay, a westerly suburb of Cowes.

The twin towns of **Cowes** lie at the mouth of the River Medina, the largest of the two being West Cowes, which is joined to East Cowes by a ferry. The appearance of the town from The Solent is a charming one, the houses rising up a well-wooded slope. The harbour is the heart of the place, while the event of the summer is the annual Cowes Regatta in August.

East of East Cowes stands Osborne House, built in the 1840s in an Italian style by the Prince Consort. The house has a fine position overlooking The Solent. It is now a hospital.

Once across the ferry and into East Cowes, the tourist can ride south-westward along the quieter east bank of the Medina past the grounds of Osborne House and later join the pretty Newport-Ryde road. At Wootton Bridge the widening creek of the same name is crossed about 1½ miles from its mouth into The Solent. A little farther on a side lane goes left into Fishbourne, a pretty corner most notable today as the departure point of a vehicular ferry to Portsmouth. To the east is Quarr Abbey which consists of a few remains only. Round about is pleasant woodland.

From the Fishbourne fork, the road climbs Quarr Hill, a useful viewpoint, and then drops steeply to climb again and enter Ryde by Queens Road and John Street and so into the High Street, well above the Esplanade and Pier.

Ryde (50) lies below and along a slope looking northward across Spithead at Portsmouth. It is familiar to tourists as the principal arrival port on the island. Many of the most important buildings lie just west of the main street, in Lind Street. Ryde is a good shopping centre, but as a touring headquarters for the cycle tourist it suffers from the same disadvantage as Cowes—it is too far from the hilly and more interesting southern coastline.

From the Esplanade Station at Ryde, a road curves round by St. John's Park and then goes leftward to Nettlestone Green before striking south-eastward by St. Helens and round the southern shore of Brading Harbour into **Bembridge** (56) a straggling resort.

The next lap of the round-island trip is towards the south west, climbing past the west side of Bembridge Down. To the east is the Yarborough Monument, an obelisk commemorating the first Earl of Yarborough. From the monument, at a height of 328 ft., there is a view across Sandown Bay to Dunnose Point and northward over Bembridge at the mainland.

Across levels the route travels past Yaverland and gains the edge of the sea before entering **Sandown** (61½), a large resort with the best stretch of sands in the Isle of Wight.

From Sandown it is a main-road journey into Shanklin (64)—

see page 58 for a description—and then comes, at the end of the journey, the hardest part of the trip.

This is by the main road which rises about 450 ft. in 1½ miles to 563 ft. above sea level. Climbing out of **Shanklin**, the old church will be seen on the right amongst trees. On forking left slightly, near the church, the ascent begins in earnest and does not slacken until it reaches the summit, after which the road runs as a shelf commanding fine views into Luccombe Chine. The final descent into **Ventnor** (68½) needs every care.

This round tour can be broken conveniently by halting for the night at either Carisbrooke youth hostel or at nearby Newport.

ACROSS THE ISLE TO CARISBROOKE CASTLE

From Ventnor or Whitwell it is a pleasant lane run northward to Newport and Carisbrooke Castle. Care should be exercised on the narrow main thoroughfares leading across the island as they are traversed by 'buses. The drivers of these are usually exemplary in their conduct and the visiting cyclist should behave similarly. Newport is a large town, the commercial capital of the island, and has a business-like air. After staying at Ventnor and visiting Carisbrooke, an hour or two amongst the streets and shops of Newport can be very refreshing.

From Ventnor the way lies first of all along the road which keeps on the top of The Undercliff and gives fine sea and cliff views from its commanding position on the upland. At an altitude of 328 ft., the road turns northward and then drops between hedgerows into **Whitwell** (3½), a large village lining both sides of the road. The youth hostel lies at the south end close to the 'bus halt at the church. The White Horse, a pleasant village inn to the left of the road, offers meals.

From Whitwell, the going is much easier as the land falls to the valley of the River Yar. After the bleakness of the upland it is pleasant to be in a countryside of small farms, little streams and distant panoramas of thrusting hill ridges.

Godshill (6½), a striking little village, stands on a knoll and its picturesque cottages and church form a composite picture which would be hard to match anywhere in the island. The church dates from the early fifteenth century.

GODSHILL

The remainder of the journey into Newport lies along an up-and-down country road by Rookley and over the railway at Blackwater into Shide with its level crossing, before coming to the metropolis of the island, Newport (11½).

Newport lies at the head of the navigable part of the River Medina and is the most workaday of the big towns on the island. Its ancient importance arose from its proximity to Carisbrooke, but today it is a shopping centre for a wide area. The colonnaded town hall dates from 1816, and not far away, in Holyrood Street, Pyle Street and Sea Street, are some interesting old houses.

Carisbrooke village and **Carisbrooke Castle** lie a mile south west. To reach the latter, the road towards Chale Green should be taken and then a fork-road to the right followed to the entrance gate of the castle. The castle dominates the surrounding landscape from its wooded hill, the most prominent features being the towered gatehouse at one end and the imposing keep at the other. The hill was used as a strongpoint from early times and was fortified by the Normans and at several periods until Elizabethan times. Its chief historical association is with Charles I, who was imprisoned there.

There is a small charge for admission. The youth hostel is at the Governor's House, actually inside the castle.

The gatehouse formerly had a removable bridge across the ditch below. The walk along the ramparts gives a comprehensive picture of the inner buildings. Carisbrooke Church is the strongest feature of the nearby village.

From the east side of Carisbrooke Castle a narrow highway heads southward past the wooded desmesne of Gatecombe House and mounts through the hamlet of Chillerton to the lonely upland once more. Then follows a steady fall to Beckfield Cross, Chale Green and Chale again, from which the outward route of the previous day is retraced as far as Niton. A left turn in the village, then a right lead through a picturesque little dale up a sharp hill into **Whitwell** (24½), from which it is a familiar run back across the downs to **Ventnor** (28).

OVER THE DOWNS

A day of any short period spent at Ventnor or Whitwell should be spent in walking. One obvious suggestion for a ramble afoot concerns Week Down, which lies between the two places.

From Ventnor a morning 'bus could be taken to Whitwell. From the 'bus stop near the church, the village street should be followed northward as far as a by-road going rightward and soon crossing the railway, before bending right to some isolated cottages and farms lying east of the village. Past a particularly miry farmyard section, the path mounts a sunken lane before meeting, unexpectedly, a fingerpost, where the way is leftward through a narrow avenue overgrown with weeds to another (and as uninformative) fingerpost. Here the way lies clearly towards the crest of the curve of Week Down. In the valley below, to the north-east, stands Wroxall, and towards the right the ugly modern houses of Upper Ventnor are laid out.

The way here is rightward along the ridge and across Ventnor golf course. The land tipples so sharply into the sea on the right that there is no suggestion of the two busy roads and the Undercliff. Nearer Ventnor, however, the end of the pier can be seen far below and the coast along as far as Dunnose Point bears a faraway look. The final drop into the upper part of Ventnor is a steep one.

This walk and 'bus ride takes about two hours. The walking part is about three miles. Ventnor can be left at breakfast time and a return made for lunch.

———————————

From Ventnor the traverse of the ridge from St. Boniface Down, behind the town, to Cook's Castle, east of Wroxall, is a longer excursion, worth a full afternoon and evening.

Near Ventnor Station a track commences the stiff climb of **St. Boniface Down**. The summit is 787 ft. above sea level and National Trust property. The side of the hilltop nearest the sea is at present disfigured by tall radar towers. The ridge can be followed along a footpath, first eastward and then towards the north. Altitude should be kept all the way and the path descending rightward into Shanklin avoided. There are line views over most of the island from the ridge, the inland prospect towards Newport being unfolded during the descent towards **Cook's Castle**, a notable viewpoint, 562 ft. above sea level. All the northern half of the island can be seen, from the Freshwater cliffs in the west to Culver Cliff in the east. Below lies Wroxall in its vee-valley, across which appears the Worsley Monument at the end of a parallel ridge, also pointing northward. To the right of this can be seen Godshill Church and, again to the right, Carisbrooke Castle.

From Cooks Castle a path curls round the edge of the hill and into **Wroxall**, from which village there is train and 'bus communication with Ventnor.

About five miles of walking is entailed in this round.

The hosteller starting at Whitwell will, of course, walk over Week Down first, seek lunch at Ventnor, and then climb over St. Boniface Down to Cook's Castle and Wroxall. If he still feels energetic and does not wish to travel by train or 'bus to Ventnor and then finish up by 'bus to Whitwell, he can walk over Week Down again from Wroxall to Whitwell, a distance of about three miles.

Cycling in the Isle of Wight today

As Harold Briercliffe wrote this cycle route guide in the late 1940s, many of the roads he mentions are now busier than they were and are not suitable for cycling today. Suggested alternative cycle routes, from Sustrans, which are in the same location as Harold's original route are listed below. To devise your own detailed route and map in the region, go to www.sustrans.org.uk/map for online mapping, and free iphone and android cycling apps.

National Cycle Network Route 23 on the Isle of Wight meanders from **Cowes** to **Sandown**. It is a largely traffic-free route on a converted railway path. From the ferry terminal at Cowes to the coast at Sandown, it is a lovely 14-mile saunter, easily achievable in a day-return trip.

Regional Route 67 provides a wonderful 60-mile circular route around the whole of the Isle of Wight on minor roads. This route passes through many of the small towns on the island and offers some fantastic sea views.

Useful maps and books (available from www.sustransshop.co.uk): *Cycle Tours Hampshire and The Isle of Wight* and *Hampshire and The Isle of Wight: Cycling Country Lanes.*

IT'S SMARTER!
IT'S STRONGER!
IT'S STREAMLINED!

ONLY

Coventry · Eagle
CYCLES

HAVE IT!

It's the new

'CLAW' SEAT STAY

A Coventry-Eagle Patent

MODELS FITTED WITH THIS FEATURE INCLUDE :— 34 & 35. £13. 19. 6.
MODELS 56 & 57. £18. 19. 6.   MODELS 58 & 59. £19. 19. 6.

★ All Coventry-Eagle Cycles are rustproofed by the Bonderising process

THE COVENTRY-EAGLE CYCLE & MOTOR CO., LTD. COVENTRY

CHAPTER III

THE NEW FOREST

EITHER as an extension of a holiday in the Isle of Wight or as a separate tourlet, an exploration of the New Forest is worthy of consideration. The forest is a great natural heritage, in many respects a survival of the England of the days before the Norman Conquest.

The area of the New Forest consists largely of woodland and open heath and is probably the finest of the large stretches of wood in England. Much of the woodland consists of comparatively recent plantings, however, and some of the country is only now beginning to recover from the ravages of wartime use. About one-third of the forest comprises private lands, the remaining 64,707 acres belonging to the Crown.

The administration of the New Forest is delegated to the Forestry Commission, acting under the direction of the Ministry of Agriculture. The Verderers, an ancient foundation, retains the grazing rights of animals. Among the attractions of the New Forest are the half-wild ponies and donkeys which are to be seen from many of the roads.

The extent of the New Forest, like that of Epping, is not great. It is easily enclosed within the triangle formed by the roads from Salisbury in the north to Christchurch in the west and from Salisbury again by Totton to Calshot Point in the south-east, the coast between Christchurch and Calshot Point forming the approximate southern limit. The greatest interest in the forest is contained within a smaller area than this, however.

Several important main roads traverse the New Forest. Perhaps the most important of these starts at Winchester and runs by Romsey to Cadnam, Ringwood and Dorchester. From this through route, which forms part of the main highway to West Dorset and East Devon from London, a fleeting impression of the scenery of the forest can be obtained. This road (A31) is exceptionally busy at holiday times. Similarly, the highway which runs parallel, a few miles to the south, and connects Southampton with Bournemouth (A35) is also busy and runs through Lyndhurst, "the capital" of the New Forest. The remaining high roads, such as that from Cadnam by Lyndhurst to Brockenhurst and Lymington, are quieter and as well surfaced. The remaining lanes vary from well-surfaced routes between villages to unmetalled and rough forest "rides". The latter form secluded routes for the exploring cyclist and give the best impression of the forest. Some of these obscure lane routes are given in the outline tour which begins on page 74.

The influence of Southampton can be felt along the eastern margin of the forest. Some of the villages here are suburbs of the city. In the west, and especially along the coast, the absorbing tendency is re-asserted with Christchurch and the eastern outlines of Bournemouth. Of the towns in the forest or close to it, Lyndhurst is central and smart, with a touch of antiquity; Brockenhurst is a charming large village which clearly belongs to the forest; Lymington is a handsome little town on an inlet of The Solent; and Beaulieu is both old and prettily situated.

Of the numerous villages, Minstead is possibly the most typical New Forest settlement, while Milford-on-Sea is a growing little resort with a pebbly beach and a good outlook across at the Isle of Wight. Lymington, a little north-east, might be used as a base for a short holiday.

Accommodation is available in most of the larger villages and towns. The forest can be explored quite readily from a point on or near the sea, and this course is recommended. Youth hostellers could spend their maximum of three nights at the Norleywood hostel, from which the tour is described. Lymington is less than three miles south-west of Norleywood which is one of the most convenient hostels in the country. It is a specially-built single-storey structure in timber and has hot-plate cooking. The accommodation is limited to 32, however, and advance booking is advisable at holiday times.

APPROACHES

The direct road from London to Southampton, for the New Forest, lies by Knightsbridge Road from Hyde Park Corner, through Kensington Gore to Hammersmith and along Chiswick

High Road to Turnham Green Church and so along the Great West Road before turning off for Staines, Egham, Virginia Water, the Bagshot by-pass, Camberley, Hook, Basingstoke, Winchester (64 miles from London), Chandler's Ford and Bassett. At Bassett, however, the congested and narrow streets of Southampton (76 miles) can be avoided by turning rightward along A35 to Redbridge and Totton. The New Forest is entered at Lyndhurst Road Station and there follow nearly three miles of glades into Lyndhurst (83), where a left turn towards the south along a straight road undulates into Brockenhurst through more woodland. Across the toll bridge at Lymington (91), along the estuary a short way and then through lanes, it is a further three miles to Norleywood (94).

An alternative approach from Southampton, shorter and quieter, is to take the steamer from Southampton to Hythe and then across Beaulieu Heath to Beaulieu. East Boldre and Norleywood (86 miles from London).

From Oxford (for cyclists from Birmingham, Manchester, Yorkshire and the North), the road (a fast one) to Winchester leads through Abingdon, Newbury and Whitchurch, a distance of 52 miles. At Winchester (for a description of the town, see pages 85–86) the route from London is joined. Winchester has a youth hostel, situated near the centre of the town, at the east end of High Street, and close to Soke Bridge.

Tourists who have been in the Isle of Wight can join this New Forest tour very readily by using the Yarmouth-Lymington ferry. The road distance between Whitwell youth hostel and Norleywood hostel is 20 miles.

Rail access to Southampton and Lymington from London is by Waterloo; Southampton is served directly, while Lymington is reached by a branch line for which the junction is Brockenhurst, which also makes a good starting place, as many of the trains on the Bournemouth line stop there.

Southampton can be reached from the Midlands and the North by through express trains.

IN THE NEW FOREST
A Two-Day Tour of 87 Miles

On leaving Norleywood youth hostel strike north-west across commons and fields and then west by Boldre to Batramsley Cross, on the main Lymington-Brockenhurst road. From here the route lies northward along A337 by one of the most graceful main-road traverses of the district into **Brockenhurst** (six miles), passing over the railway.

The small town of Brockenhurst is now almost entirely modern, but it is a pleasant halting place and is surrounded by woodland. The church, south-east of the place, was mentioned in the Domesday Book. Only a small part of the church as it now stands dates back to Saxon times, however.

Beyond the village street, the tourist should go through the watersplash (or over the adjoining bridge) and then turn leftward along a field road which soon enters Rhinefield Walk, where thickly wooded land is encountered. Neat Rhinefield Rouse the track— which is of cart-width and quite ridable with a bicycle—crosses the Ober Water and turns northward. After another stream, the Black Water, the route traverses the Vinney Ridge Ornamental Drive, a splendid avenue of rhododendrons and matured fir.

The Knightwood Oak the largest tree in the New Forest.

Soon the route crosses the Lyndhurst-Christchurch road and, bending north-west again, enters the Knightwood Enclosure, which contains some of the finest trees in the New Forest.

Some yards along the track, a sign indicates the way, rightward, to the **Knightwood Oak** (11). Bicycles should be left near the sign and the tree visited. It is a large and venerable growth, the most surprising feature being its girth. A wooden fence now protects the oak.

The route from here keeps a north-westerly direction and comes to a gateway into Mark Ash Wood. The surface is rougher than previously and as the track climbs it enters a grove of scattered beech trees—perhaps the finest beeches in the forest. In this remote corner it is sometimes possible to see wild deer, but the animals are very timid and the slightest noise sends them bounding away through the glades. Wild horses and donkeys are more commonly seen.

The track still climbs and then enters the Arboretum, a show place of cultivated firs. Yet another gateway gives access to the by-road between Lyndhurst and Fritham Cross, where this is tending strongly towards the north. A little way onward, this lane meets the busy Poole-Ringwood-Romsey highway, A31.

Here one way is rightward for about 1½ miles to the high ground of Stoney Cross Plain, where there is a disused aerodrome and facilities for snack meals. Stoney Cross is 372 ft. above sea level and one of the highest parts of the New Forest. From this neighbourhood, looking in a southerly direction, the outlook is over the undulating tops of the trees, which seem to form a carpet reaching down to the sea. On a clear day the Isle of Wight can be seen beyond the Solent. It is worthwhile going to this point and then retracing, to the by-lane indicated in the next paragraph.

The New Forest round, however, continues very shortly after meeting the main road down a by-lane striking northward and signposted "Fritham". Beyond the "Royal Oak", in Fritham, lies Eyeworth and the tree-fringed lake called Irons Well. From here a rough track goes, generally, northward through Eyeworth and Studley Woods to the Fordingbridge-Cadnam road (B3078). This attractive side-road must then be followed rightward towards the south-east and downhill nearly into the picturesque village of **Brook** (26).

Instead of entering the village, however, turn rightward and southward along a lane which eventually leads along a forest road and over a ford to the clearing near the modern Sir Walter Tyrrell Hotel (which provides meals) in which stands the **Rufus Stone** (28). The stone lies to the right of the road—the hotel is on the left—and marks the traditional spot where William II was killed. The stone had been badly damaged with the passing of the years. It is now encased in iron with the original inscription embossed thereon.

From the stone a steep rise goes uphill by Malwood to a main road (A31). On reaching this, the way is leftward, but very quickly the traffic is forsaken along a lane turning rightward into Minstead (29).

Minstead is one of the most interesting villages in the New Forest. Its delightful cottages, built on a slope, descend to the unusual little church, which stands on a hill of its own. The church is built like a cottage, with gabled windows peeping out of its roof, and a small timber spire. Like that at Brockenhurst, it was mentioned in the Domesday Book. A heavy, ancient door hangs in the twelfth century doorway and inside is a rarity, a three-decker pulpit, together with oak pews and double-tiered galleries. Near the church is an old inn—"The Trusty Servant."

From Minstead a picturesque forest lane leads southward by Manor Wood and then eastward into **Lyndhurst** (35), "the capital of the New Forest".

At the western end of the interesting main street of Lyndhurst stands the King's House, built in the reign of Charles II. Permits for camping in the New Forest are issued here. Next door is the Verderers Hall, also worth visiting. Lyndhurst is a useful stopping place for meals.

The next part of the tour commences in an easterly direction but at the Grand Hotel bends rightward towards the south-east along the Beaulieu Road. After about two miles of open country, the road bears rightward downhill and crosses a stream ("Matley Bog"). As the Beaulieu highway climbs it swings leftward. Here, an untarred road goes straight ahead and passes sandpits as it makes for Denny Lodge and through the Denny Lodge Enclosure, beyond which it is crossed by the main railway line from Southampton to Bournemouth, and gains a better road at Lady Cross. The route here is leftward and

**Typical Thames-side scenery where the
Chilterns meet the river.**

**Looking down the picturesque High Street
of Burford, Oxfordshire.**

Godshill village in the Isle of Wight.

The Rufus Stone, in a New Forest clearing.

At Friday Street, a favourite resort near Leith Hill, Surrey.

**The Long Man of Wilmington, a hillside carving on the
South Downs.**

The picturesque harbour at Rye, Sussex.

**The ancient bridge over the River Medway
at Aylesford, Kent.**

eastward along B3055 to Hatchet Pond (41), so named because of its shape. The pond has a depth of 40 ft. Refreshments are available in the vicinity.

The next section leads over open common and down into **Beaulieu** (43). The townlet is a pretty one, lying close to the Beaulieu River, and has the remains of a Cistercian Abbey on the north-east side of the bridge.

A short way back along B3054 (the road used entering Beaulieu), a lane runs leftward and in a little over two miles reaches **Bucklers Hard**. This is a small village, consisting of two rows of cottages lining a street which dips down to the river estuary. The village was once a busy shipbuilding centre, using the forest oaks. Now, however, it is a quiet place, although it saw a good deal of activity during Hitler's War. Pleasant walks lead along the river banks and are worth following without a bicycle.

From Bucklers Hard quiet lanes go southward to St. Leonards, where there is a fine old barn, and then westward to Sowley Pond, an artificial sheet which is the home of much wildlife. Two miles of easy going lead back by East End to South Baddesley and Norleywood and its youth hostel again (47).

This round introduces the tourist to the best of the varied scenery of the New Forest. If the round of 4 miles is too much for one day, as well it might be, because there is so much of interest to see, the youth hostel at Burley, about four miles east of Ringwood, could be used for a night.

Those staying for three nights at Norleywood could make a "lazy" second day by exploring the lanes leading down to the sea at Milford and at Barton and by going on to **Christchurch**, where there is a Saxon priory church, and into **Bournemouth**, a busy and attractive resort. This makes a day of about 40 miles return.

On the fringes of the New Forest and easily visited when travelling to it or in a day-ride from a centre in the forest are several historic towns and places which cannot be treated adequately in a guide which must always try to be brief.

The most notable is **Winchester**, on the London-Southampton road. The outstanding feature of this old town is the cathedral, which has a nave reputed to be the longest in Europe. In Saxon times, Winchester was virtually the capital of England. Here the Anglo-Saxon Chronicle was compiled and in the cathedral are relies of Egbert, Ethelwulf, Canute and William Rufus. The college, a lovely place, was founded by William of Wykeham. The County Hall is the sole remnant of the castle. The city (which has youth hostel and other accommodation) ought to be explored afoot.

Ringwood, on the western edge of the New Forest, was originally a Roman military post. The River Avon glides through a shallow valley hereabouts and has many pretty reaches.

Wimborne Minster, farther to the south-west, is situated where the Rivers Allen and Stour meet. The most notable building is the Minster Church, which is Norman, with an Early English chancel. The clock in the west tower has a performing figure.

Salisbury is most noteworthy for its cathedral tower, which is 404 ft. high and the tallest in England. The style is Early English. On Salisbury Plain, to the north, is Stonehenge, the world-famous prehistoric temple of unknown antiquity. The great stones forming Stonehenge were brought to the site from a distance. Salisbury Plain is crossed by exposed roads and is used to a great extent for military training.

Cycling in the New Forest today

As Harold Briercliffe wrote this cycle route guide in the late 1940s, many of the roads he mentions are now busier than they were and are not suitable for cycling today. Suggested alternative cycle routes, from Sustrans, which are in the same location as Harold's original route are listed below. To devise your own detailed route and map in the region, go to www.sustrans.org.uk/map for online mapping, and free iphone and android cycling apps.

National Cycle Network Route 2 runs through the New Forest and well beyond on a combination of forest tracks, minor roads and a converted railway path. A nice stretch to follow is from **Christchurch** through the New Forest via **Brockenhurst** on to **Hythe ferry port**, which is roughly 27 miles. Please note National Route 2 is not open or signed for about 2 miles south of Brockenhurst.

Useful maps and books (available from www.sustransshop.co.uk): *Cycle Tours Hampshire and The Isle of Wight Cycle Tours* and *Hampshire and The Isle of Wight: Cycling Country Lanes.*

Explore the Countryside

Free itineraries and route books — expert technical advice — the C.T.C. Handbook and Guide — *The C.T.C. Gazette* by post every month. These benefits enable C.T.C. members to cycle

Easily and Cheaply

They pay less for maps, receive free third-party insurance, are members of their local association with social and clubroom facilities.

"Under 18s" pay only 6s., and "Under 21s" only 10s. a year but receive all the advantages for which older members gladly pay 12s. 6d. The entrance fee is 1s.

CYCLISTS' TOURING CLUB
3 Craven Hill, London W.2

CHAPTER IV

BETWEEN LONDON AND
THE SOUTH COAST

THE roads between London and Southampton (for the New Forest) and Portsmouth (for the Isle of Wight) have already been mentioned in previous chapters. The purpose of this chapter is to deal briefly with the main routes and their alternatives between the capital and the coast of Sussex and Kent. The subject is too large to be treated fully in a short survey, but some notice is necessarily given to the wayside attractions of the dozen or more avenues leading to the sea, the Straits of Dover, and the Thames Estuary.

As a tour of the South Coast and Downs follows in the next chapter, the present survey deals only with the main arteries and does not dwell greatly on the suburbanised belt which stretches for perhaps 20 miles southward from London. This belt has its pockets of interest, but they are mainly for the leisurely evening wanderer who lives nearby, and not for the holidaymaker.

The information in this chapter should be used in conjunction with the chart on page 2. The starting point in most cases is Hyde Park Corner.

TO PORTSMOUTH

By Knightsbridge and Fulham Road to Putney Bridge, Kingston by-pass, Esher, Guildford, Godalming, Milford, Hindhead, Liphook, Petersfield, Horndean, Cosham by-pass, and into **Portsmouth**.

The 72 miles of the Portsmouth Road are perhaps the finest, scenically, of any main road between London and the South Coast. Its finest part is around **Hindhead**, but even as far as Guildford the influence of London's suburbia can be felt. **Guildford** on the main Portsmouth line, is a useful starting point for those who can take railway from London. There is a constant service of fast trains.

The part of the road beyond Petersfield is no more than pleasant, while the final miles into Portsmouth, from Horndean, are largely residential.

Esher has a pleasant green and thereafter there are commons and parks all the way through Cobham and into Guildford, the county town of Surrey. The narrow and steep High Street is one of the most picturesque in the country. Near the middle stands the Town Hall, dating from 1682, which has a projecting clock. Near the highest point of the High Street is the Abbot's Hospital, a turreted building dating back 300 years. On Stag Hill, just north-west of the town, is the modern cathedral, commenced in 1936 and now (1949) well on the way to completion.

Just south of Guildford, St. Catherine's Hill can be seen on the left surmounted by a fourteenth-century chapel. Nearby runs the **Pilgrims' Way**, which goes from Winchester to Canterbury. This Way lies along all sorts of old and modern routes, but can be traced over much of its length by the cyclist.

Godalming, based on a quaint town on the River Wey, is now largely modernised. A tributary of the Wey is next followed into Milford, after which the open wastes of Witley Common are traversed and the route begins to give some promise of the beauty to come. The road next begins to climb southward up the slope towards Hindhead. The best views are to the east, across a patchwork of woods and fields.

Hindhead is now National Trust property. The view from its 895 feet is far-reaching. It is, however, a place best visited during the week, as on Saturdays and Sundays it is a halting-place for vehicles of all kinds. The name of Gibbet Hill is attached to the summit and derives from the murder of a sailor in the eighteenth century and the fate of those responsible. **The Devil's Punch Bowl** is the name of a depression on the north side of the hill.

The country on both sides of the road is worth exploration. **Haslemere**, to the south-east, is a London suburb in splendid, wooded country, and has been called "the stockbrokers' retreat". The National Trust owns much of the land in the vicinity of Hindhead.

The road soon begins to drop steadily over Bramshott Common and enters **Liphook**, after which it mounts again to a ridge extending towards the south-west.

Petersfleld is a pleasant country town at the head of the River Rother. Beyond the town, the highway lifts again, this time up Butser Hill, traversing open downland before dropping into Horndean and on through busy Waterlooville. Then, over the ridge of Portsdown, it by-passes Cosham and crosses Portsbridge Creek to Portsea Island, on which **Portsmouth** lies.

TO CHICHESTER

At Milford (see opposite), on the main Portsmouth Road beyond Guildford, the road to Chichester breaks off leftward and leads, beyond the latter town, to the low peninsula which terminates at Selsey Bill. This route is quieter than the main road, to which it is an alternative if the route westward from Chichester to Portsmouth is taken, or, better, the lane route westward from Mid Lavant through West Stoke to Funtington, Westbourne and Havant, thus avoiding the busy highway from Chichester to Portsmouth by Emsworth.

This road to Chichester leads through some of the finest parts of West Sussex, after Haslemere, and beyond that town has on the left the solitudes of Blackdown, a high wooded tract which deserves careful exploration. There is a steep climb across a small range and then comes **Midhurst**, useful as a halting place, after which the South Downs are pierced at a most beautiful hollow and then follows an easy run across the coastal levels into Chichester.

From Guildford the main Portsmouth road is followed to the outskirts of Milford, where a left fork goes along A286 and through wooded country into **Haslemere**, a small town originally but now a residential suburb. The road keeps to high ground as it crosses Marley Common, leaving to the left the heights of **Blackdown** (918 ft.). The view eastward across the Weald of Sussex is a wide and varied one.

Beyond the crossroad village of Fernhurst, the route reaches Cooksbridge and begins the climb by Henley Common and round two sweeping bends to a summit 500 ft. above sea level. The subsequent fall into Midhurst is straight and easy.

Midhurst, in the gracious valley of the River Rother, is a large village or townlet. To the east lies Cowdray Park, where there are the remains of a Tudor mansion and splendid riverside and woodland scenery.

Three miles beyond Midhurst, the highway rises steadily. Approaching Cocking, the bold spur of Linch Down becomes prominent to the right and next a low pass (345 ft.) is traversed with the railway, and Singleton is reached. From Singleton a charming lane rambles below the foot of the South Downs to the Duncton-Chichester road near Upper Waltham (see opposite).

The country becomes more level as Chichester is reached through Mid Lavant.

Chichester is a small city of Roman origin. The cathedral dates from 1090 and is 376 ft. long. One of the best viewpoints in Chichester is to be gained from the North Walls, a walk skirting the line of the City Walls.

For Selsey Bill, the road leading southward past the station must be followed. The coast is flat and has sand dunes and bungalow towns. West Wittering, with its south-westerly outlook towards the Isle of Wight, is perhaps more to the liking of the tourist. Selsey Bill is nine miles from Chichester.

TO CHICHESTER (AND PORTSMOUTH) BY PETWORTH

An alternative route to Chichester lies to the east of that by Midhurst and passes through Petworth. It is a quieter road to the coast than either of the two routes described previously and is probably the quietest of all the main highways leading from the west side of London to the sea. It starts, like the Midhurst route, at Milford, but has no Haslemere to break its tranquility. On it there are only small towns and villages and from it the rolling Weald—the belt between the North Downs and the South Downs—appears at its most picturesque and varied. On both sides of the route, beyond Wormley Hill (south of Milford) and almost into Chichester, the lanes are worth exploration. Petworth is the outstanding man-made feature of the highway (A283) and the grandest natural feature is Duncton Hill.

From Milford, the route leads southward along an up-and-down road by Wormley Hill and into **Chiddingfold**, a roadside village built around a green. Until the rise of modern industry, Sussex was an iron-smelting area, the hammers in the forges being driven by water power. The "hammer ponds" which abound in this district derive from the industry.

North Chapel is a streamside village, beyond which higher ground is traversed. The district seen to the west around Lurgashall, has some attractive lanes and valleys.

Petworth is one of the showplaces of Sussex, with narrow streets and old houses. There is a Mid-European air about the place. Petworth House and Park, to the west, are both delightful.

At Coultershaw Bridge a narrow belt of greensand soil is encountered and on it flourish evergreens, forming a dark foreground to the smoothly moulded summits of the South Downs seen ahead. The highway lifts above the meadows through the rambling "village street" of Duncton and then in an impressive curve to the right mounts sharply through the woods up **Duncton Hill**. The hilltop is shrouded in trees and there is a quarry, so that the most impressive views are to the right and north-westward through the branches about 300 yards from the summit.

The foothill roads on the north side of the Downs lead through and to charming villages, notably East Lavington and Graffham to the west and Sutton and Bignor to the west. At Bignor there are the remains of a Roman villa.

From the summit of Duncton Hill the main road slides smoothly into a bare, treeless hollow and by the hamlet of Upper Waltham, where an alluring little lane runs under the slopes to Singleton (see also opposite). The main route climbs a steady rise to a hilltop cross roads. Here a lane goes rightward and leads along a ridge top in three miles to **Goodwood** racecourse, the most beautifully situated of all racecourses in Britain. The busy time here is the last week in July. The route by Goodwood to Chichester forms an alternative to the main road.

The through road continues downhill through a vast forest, some of it in the hands of the Forestry Commission, and emerges on the line of the Roman Stane Street which leads south-west and into Chichester.

TO ARUNDEL (FOR BOGNOR OR LITTLEHAMPTON)

Hyde Park Corner is left as indicated on page 89 and the route continued by Putney Bridge to the Kingston by-pass, along which a left turn leads southward by Hook to Leatherhead. Then follow Capel, Kingsfold, Billingshurst, Pulborough, Bury and Arundel.

The road to Arundel and the coast to the south of it is, on the whole, an easy one. Beyond Leatherhead the road keeps close to the winding River Mole and passes distinctive **Box Hill**. After Dorking, the northerly spurs of Leith Hill fill the view on the left and soon, as the highway runs south and then south-west, the fine southern face of Leith Hill itself can be seen dominating the low-lying Weald. The run across the Weald is pleasant enough, but has no outstanding features. Billingshurst is a straggling main-road town on the line of the Stane Street and it is not until Pulborough that there is much of interest to notice.

Pulborough lies amongst the water meadows near the confluence of the Arun and the Rother, while farther ahead Bury and Amberley (both east of the road) are attractive villages. A short climb to a ridge and a steady fall lead into **Arundel**, one of the most interesting towns in the South of England.

There is nothing calling for special mention along the route until **Leatherhead**, now becoming a suburb but based on an old town. The next few miles are pretty enough in their combination of wood, water and the slopes of the North Downs, through which river and road wriggle. The builder, however, has been active here, too. Beyond a particularly charming curve in river and highway, a by-pass keeps west of the old road and crosses the Mole at Burford Bridge, where Keats is said to have worked on 'Endymion'. To the left rises Box Hill, with steep slopes and public footpaths, now saved by the National Trust from spoliation. There is no need to enter Dorking, which is skirted by a through road on the east.

Dorking, situated amongst the finest scenery in Surrey, was originally a small market town. Tourists wishing to make a detour from the main route should pass through the town and along South Street then take the by-road climbing rightward through Redlands

Wood to Coldharbour village which stands amongst pine trees and has wide prospects towards the south and south-east.

The road curves round the southern face of **Leith Hill** and from it the summit can be gained. This is 965 ft. above sea level and the highest point south of London. From the tower there are widespread views, stretching from London in the north to the Channel in the south. Again, much of the summit is owned by the National Trust.

A little farther west a side road slopes steeply downhill to the south, and at the pleasing village of Ockley regains the main route, here labelled A29.

After by-passing Dorking, the through route runs in farming country, mostly along Static Street, into Billingshurst, close to which, at Pear Tree Farm, most of the work of Frank Patterson, the cycling artist, has been done.

There is a sharp rise and fall before **Pulborough**, a townlet of stone buildings and gardens on ground raised slightly above the marshes of the River Arun. These are crossed on the way by Hardham, with its scanty remains of a priory, to the outskirts of Bury. The shapely outline of the South Downs now surges across the sky. On the levels to the left is Amberley (see page 120) and behind the village lift the bare, whalebacked downs. Closer are the tree-fringed crests of Westburton and Bignor Hills, up a spur of which the road climbs sharply to Whiteways Lodge at 420 ft., beyond which it falls alongside the ducal splendours of Arundel Park into **Arundel** (see page 117), which has a splendid situation where the hills end and the levels begin.

Riders making direct for Bognor can turn right at Whiteways Lodge for Eastergate and Bognor. Littlehampton lies four miles south of Arundel (see page 117).

TO WORTHING

The road from London to Worthing is identical with that to Arundel as far as Kingsfold, south of Dorking. Then the route is Horsham, Ashington, Findon, Broadwater and Worthing.

Like the Arundel road, the one to Worthing cuts across the Weald, but there is not a great deal of noteworthy scenery until the South

Downs are seen from the high ground approaching Ashington. Here the dominating feature is the hilltop clump of trees at Chanctonbury Ring (see opposite); which forms a prominent landmark on the bare line of the Downs towards the south-east. Between Ashington and Washington there is a piece of miniature beauty as the greensand belt is crossed, the road winding between pines and gardens. Beyond Washington, there is a brief climb to a gap through the Downs. Findon, the next village, is by-passed and thereafter all the way into Worthing is largely surbanised.

From Kingsfold, the Horsham and Worthing road reaches **Horsham** in four miles. Horsham, 37 miles from London and in the north of Sussex, is nevertheless the county town. It is a pleasant place and, with its modern shops and suburbs, more like a Surrey town than one in inland Sussex. Horsham has a thirteenth-century church—and a railway station which is well served by expresses between London and the coast.

St. Leonard's Forest, stretching for some miles east of Horsham as far as the main Brighton Road and even beyond that, as the Tilgate and Worth Forests, is a wilderness of wood, heath and preserved land. It makes a good day-run from London, a quiet approach from Dorking (see page 94) being along a by-lane starting from Deepdene, east of the town, and then running via Newdigate, Rusper, Faygate Station to Beacon Hill, 473 ft. above sea level. From Colgate, nearby, a lane runs eastward to the main Brighton Road at Pease Pottage, south of Crawley (page 98).

After Horsham, the Worthing road is uneventful, for some way, except for a sharp rise just south of the town. Beyond the potteries and station at Southwater, an obvious lane alternative, going rightward, forms a pleasant break from the main road as far as Dial Post.

The main highway climbs to Dial Post from a pretty dip, to the west of which is Knapp Castle and a curving lake. **Dial Post** has become a cyclists' rendezvous since 1948, when Mr. and Mrs. George Farrant, formerly keen club cyclists in Surrey, established themselves at "The Gables", a large house to the left of the road.

They have transformed the premises into a pleasant calling-place for wheelfolk, largely because they know what the tourist needs and can give it to him.

Beyond Dial Post comes a stretch of meadowland and then the tree-crowned ridge of **Chanctonbury Ring** begins to arrest the eye (see also pages 121–22) on the downs to the left. **Ashington** straggles down a slight slope dipping to a stream, from which there is a climb and fall before road and stream keep company on a picturesque rise through the greensand into **Washington**.

The rise to the gap through the Downs is a short one and soon the tourist is following a wide, shallow valley in the chalk into Findon, the closest village to Cissbury Ring (see page 122), which is about 1½ miles east. A by-pass skirts the village on the west side and then it is villas for much of the way into Worthing. Naturalists will remember that at Broadwater, a mile out of Worthing, are buried Richard Jefferies and W. H. Hudson.

TO BRIGHTON (VIA HORSHAM)

An alternative route to Brighton, via Horsham, goes south east from Horsham, through quiet country, along A281, by Cowfold and Henfield. This is a useful link for cyclists living in south-west London and for visitors from the north-west travelling to Brighton by Oxford and Guildford. Horsham-Brighton, 23 miles.

TO BRIGHTON

From Hyde Park Corner, southward by Grosvenor Place, Grosvenor Gardens, Victoria, Vauxhall Bridge Road, Vauxhall Bridge, Kennington Oval, Brixton Road, Brixton Hill, Streatham, Croydon by-pass (right, or west, of Croydon), Purley, Redhill, Crawley (or by-pass) Handcross, Pyecombe, Brighton.

This is the main road to Brighton, along A23, a hilly and busy road which has the influence of London about it for most of its 52 miles. Once, the tram terminus at Purley might have marked the end of London, but nowadays Redhill, Horley and Crawley (which is 30 miles along the road) are suburbs, as, indeed, is Brighton. Farther south than Crawley, A23 would have been more of a suburban road had the railway been nearer. As it is, development has centred on Haywards Heath and Burgess Hill, to the east, leaving Cuckfield on its hill as a more natural country town.

As far as Crawley, the road is a wearying one, and building development is common enough as the road threads its way through the chalk downs. The Weald is at its best on this route after Crawley and particularly about Handcross. Afterwards, it is more ordinary until the South Downs are traversed through a characteristic valley by Pyecombe and Pangdean before the gradual descent to the sea at Brighton.

The start of the run from London is commonplace and there are few glimpses of open spaces for many miles, Streatham Common being one of them. At Thornton Heath Pond (the pond lies to the right of the road), a by-pass strikes rightward and goes by Purley Way and the Croydon Airport, past which it climbs before dropping rather smartly into Purley.

From Thornton Heath Pond the main, tram-lined, route passes along the congested main street of **Croydon**, a large town 11 miles from London which contrives to retain independence of the Metropolis, despite its proximity. Croydon, like all the district immediately south and east of London, was badly battered from the air during the 1939-45 war. The town and the south London suburbs which extend northward from it have perhaps more enthusiastic racing and touring cyclists than any other district in the country. It has within its area the Herne Hill track, there are many large and enthusiastic clubs, and some of the best-known cyclists in Britain live in the district.

The old route rejoins the new at Purley.

The way to go at Purley crossroads is rightward, through the chalk downs and by Merstham into **Redhill,** the modern twin of Reigate to the west. **Horley** has little to detain the cyclist, but at **Crawley** there is an interesting old inn, the George, as well as catering places for the cyclist. Crawley is a normal halt for cyclists making for Brighton on week-end and day runs.

Instead of going through Crawley, the by-pass to the west can be used. This takes a wide sweep, however, and it is preferable to go through the town.

Once out of Crawley the road becomes more interesting as it climbs through Tilgate Forest and so to Handcross, which is 504 ft. above sea level and is an important junction. Leftward a side road strikes off for Cuckfield, Haywards Heath and Lewes (see page 101). After the steep drop down Handcross Hill the main road traverses a stretch of country without any large roadside towns and later begins to climb between the downland humps of Wolstonbury Hill and Newtimber Hill before running through a shallow valley and dropping into Brighton.

TO EASTBOURNE

East of the main Brighton Road stretches a hilly and varied tract of country which provides, to the south of East Grinstead, a splendid touring ground, becoming wild and well-wooded in Ashdown Forest. Along A22, the main Eastbourne Road, the western side of the forest appears to advantage. At Forest Row, three miles south-east of East Grinstead, an alternative route strikes off to the east of the main road, rejoining at Maresfield after a hillier course.

After the descent from the crest of Ashdown Forest at Wych Cross, the scenery is quieter, more wealden, in character, as A22 reaches Uckfield, a pleasant country town, and then skirts **Halisham** (see page 103) in a flatter district before gaining the surbanised area around Polegate and Willingdon, to the west of which rise the familiar whalebacks of the South Downs. Eastbourne proper is encountered near the railway station, beyond which lies The Parade and the sea.

From Hyde Park Corner the route goes to Kennington Oval, Streatham, Croydon (or by-pass) and Purley as indicated on page 97).

On emerging from the Croydon by-pass at Purley, the Eastbourne road goes straight ahead and traverses the Caterham Valley, with it sides lined with houses. Past Caterham the highway keeps between chalk downs before descending into **Godstone**, a large and pleasant village. South of the village there is a hilly alternative to the main road, which keeps to lower ground on the east. At Blindley Heath a by road goes leftward into **Lingfield**, a pleasant small town with a large church testifying to former importance. More wooded country appears past Blindley Heath and the New Chapel crossroads (see below) to Felbridge, where Sussex is entered and the highway commences to climb into **East Grinstead**, a charming country town which is growing into another piece of suburbia. Its wide main street and timber-built houses are redolent of a former day.

After East Grinstead, A22 undulates to Forest Row, thereafter starts the steady rise to **Wych Cross** and the open heaths and woodlands of Ashdown Forest. Pleasant side roads go off westward towards **West Hoathly**, in a delightful district of ridges and little valleys. The A22 falls from the ridge to undulate past Nutley and Maresfield and into Uckfield. Then the going is across lower country, by East Hoathly. Leftward is a rural area traversed by pretty lanes.

Hailsham (see page 103) lies east of the main road, which continues past Polegate junction, along the Willingdon bypass and down the last long fall into Eastbourne.

TO BRIGHTON (VIA NEW CHAPEL)

A quieter and more interesting route to Brighton than the main road by Handcross can be found by using the preceding route to Eastbourne as far as New Chapel, three miles north of East Grinstead.

By going rightward at New Chapel, along B2028, some pleasant going is found by Crawley Down and Turners Hill. Then a long projecting tongue of a southward-pointing ridge is followed which descends into field-and-brook country before gaining Lindfield, Haywards Heath, Burgess Hill, and Hassocks—all modern places close to the main railway line between London and Brighton. The final stretch leads by Clayton and through the chalk to Pangdean, on the main London-Brighton road about six miles north of Brighton.

Lewes.

TO LEWES, NEWHAVEN AND SEAFORD

Another important spur road strikes rightward off the Eastbourne road at Wych Cross (see opposite) and then drops through a gracious, thinly-populated district past Sheffield Park to reach the strategic gap where Lewes stands amongst the bold chalk hills of the South Downs. **Lewes** is described fully on page 125.

A busy main road runs on the west side of the River Ouse between the hills and the marshes and comes to the Channel port of Newhaven. A quieter lane route follows the east side and skirts the foot of the downs before running into the modern resort of **Seaford** (see page 125).

LONDON TO EASTBOURNE (BY TUNBRIDGE WELLS)

Another, longer, route between London and Eastbourne lies through Tunbridge Wells. This goes from Hyde Park Corner to Kennington Oval as indicated previously and then follows Camberwell New

Road, Camberwell Green, Denmark Hill, Dulwich, Crystal Palace, Penge and Bromley, gaining the open country at Locks Bottom, beyond Bromley Common.

The country onwards is varied and hilly, especially as it crosses the high ridge on which stands Heathfield (see page 130). Between Heathfield and Hailsham the country is well forested and there are many useful loop routes for the explorer.

Beyond Locks Bottom the main road (A21) follows a bypass round Farnborough (on the right) and also misses Green Street Green (on the left). Thereafter there is a steady climb up a green valley to Knockholt Station, after which a little pass is traversed at 448 ft. above sea level. The route keeps to high ground for about 1½ miles, reaching the summit at 562 ft. at Polhill. From this point there is a good view southward across the Darent Valley at the wooded ridges beyond Sevenoaks.

There follows a drop to Dunton Green and Riverhead, after which Tubs Hill is climbed into **Sevenoaks**, an old and pleasant town now partly a London dormitory. The houses in the High Street include some with attractive gardens. A mile south-east of Sevenoaks stands Knole Park, which is open to the public. The house is one of the oldest baronial mansions in England.

Riverhill, leading south from Sevenoaks, is even steeper than Tubs Hill and after crossing well-tilled farming country **Tonbridge** is reached, seven miles from Sevenoaks. Tonbridge is a market town on the River Medway, close to which are the remains of a castle.

Six more uneventful miles lead by Southborough to Tunbridge Wells.

Tunbridge Wells is a resort in an open situation close to the border between Kent and Sussex. Its springs have been noted since the seventeenth century for their health-giving properties. There are many attractive walks over the heathland in the neighbourhood. The chief feature of the town is The Pantiles, a short parade dating from 1638. One side has a colonnade, the other lime trees. Towards the west are weathered—and much visited—sandstone outcrops.

The suburbs extend for some way south, but thereafter the country becomes wilder, with forest and heath alternating. Saxonbury Hill, with a 1,000-year-old camp, is ascended to the summit at 576 ft. To the east lies Wadhurst, which has "gravestones" made of wealden iron. The road keeps to high ground past Mark Cross, but undulates before **Mayfield**, a charming village with timbered houses and more iron slabs, this time in the church pavement. The next few miles are hilly and twisting and there are many fine short-distance views. At Cross-in-Hand the Heathfield ridge is followed east for a short way before the road plunges down steeply by woodlands and fields to the marshes and to Horsebridge and **Hailsham**, an important road centre and market town. To the west, in low country on the banks of the River Cuckmere, are the ruins of Michelham Priory.

Beyond Hailsham, this route to Eastbourne reaches Pole gate junction, from which the road to the sea is indicated on pages 130 by the Willingdon by-pass.

TO BATTLE AND HASTINGS

From Tonbridge, the Hastings road strikes away south-east from the Heathfield and Eastbourne road and past Pembury keeps to a high island of ridge country commanding wide views. There is a fall into Lamberhurst, a pleasant village which was once a centre of the smelting trade. The countryside is a varied one all the way by Flimwell and Hurst Green, to the east of which is **Bodiam** and its castle. The castle is now owned by the National Trust. It dates from the fourteenth century and while now no more than a shell, it is impressive because of its wide moat and great gateway on the north side.

Robertsbridge is a pleasant halting place. Two miles farther on an alternative route along B2091 goes left for Hastings, avoiding Battle.

Battle, on the main road, is a picturesque town. At the foot of the main street is the long, imposing gateway of Battle Abbey, founded by William the Conqueror in fulfilment of a vow made before the Battle of Hastings. The Decorated gateway dates from the fourteenth century. The abbey ruins may be visited on most days. From the terrace inside the grounds there is a view south-westward across the site of the battle to the heights of Senlac and Telhamwhere the Normans camped before the battle. The strongpoint at Battle was held by Harold.

The Hastings highway continues southward along the Telham ridge, passing through the inland suburb of Hollington and by Bohemia Road into the town. St. Leonards-on-Sea lies towards the west. Still farther west is **Bexhill**, which can be reached along by-lanes going westward and southward from Battle, through Catsfield.

TO RYE

North-east of Hastings the Sussex and Kent coast consists mainly of featureless marshes, some of them in military hands. There is no through road to Rye, for instance, which forms the western approach to the area. However, the tourist wishing to reach Rye (description on page 131) for the Walland and Romney Marshes can avoid the busy main road through Maidstone (see opposite) by adopting the first part of the Hastings road as far as Flimwell.

From Flimwell, a secondary road numbered A268 wanders pleasantly towards the south-east by Field Green, Sandhurst, Newenden and Peasmarsh and so into Rye.

TO FOLKESTONE

From London Bridge the route goes first along the Old Kent Road to New Cross and then past New Cross Station to Lewisham High Road. From Lewisham the way lies along Lee High Road to Lee Green, beyond which right for the Sidcup by-pass and Foots Cray. Not until Farningham, 20 miles from London, does the road cease to be suburban. The village is by-passed but it is traversed by an alternative—the old—route.

The North Downs are crossed by Wrotham Hill and the next stage consists of up-and-down going into Maidstone. Beyond Maidstone the road keeps in the valley of the River Den, gradually climbing between the long line of the North Downs on the left and the Quarry Hills. Ashford is a large railway town, and thereafter to Hythe, Sandgate and Folkestone is more commonplace.

From the Farningham by-pass the country becomes rural and after the first two-mile rise the upland is gained at Kingsdown. The highest point, at the top of Wrotham Hill, is about six miles from Farningham and touches 726 ft. above sea level. Just beyond the summit there is a splendid view southward over the Weald of Kent. The best picture is in April and May when the fruit orchards are in bloom. The southern face of Wrotham Hill is steep. Halfway down, the Pilgrims' Way crosses the road—the Way is a mere track hereabouts. Wrotham (say "Rootham") is a townlet with a fine church and old houses. It can be by-passed. Past Wrotham Heath A20 begins to run eastward with the railway.

Just east, a by-road route commences on the right. It goes over a level crossing and then enters **Offham**, which has the only quintain post in England. A quintain is a tilting-pole. The village is otherwise uninteresting.

This alternative route continues into Teston, where the deep valley of the River Medway has to be crossed, and then climbs to the north side of a ridge ("Cox Hill") before crossing the Maidstone-Headcorn road just north of **Sutton Valence**, a picturesque village, worth a detour. The alternative route keeps to high ground by Platts Heath and rejoins the main road at Lenham.

The main road beyond Wrotham Heath passes near West Mailing and comes close to the River Medway.

A lane route going north of Maidstone strikes off to the left by Aylesford, at the only permanent bridge on the Medway, between Maidstone and Rochester. Aylesford Bridge is a picturesque, narrow structure dating from the fourteenth century. The village, too, is picturesque. The alternative north of Maidstone goes over all cross-roads, passing Sandling and Bearsted before gaining the main road, A20 about three miles beyond Maidstone.

The route along A20 leaves Preston Hall, the British Legion village, to the left before dropping to Maidstone bridge and entering Maidstone town. **Maidstone** is the capital and farming centre of Kent. Its hop gardens are famous and in September are at their busiest.

The next stretch of road is noteworthy for its constant prospect of the great whaleback of the North Downs to the left. As the valley of the River Len is climbed the hills draw in closer. About 5½ miles from Maidstone, look out on the right for **Leeds Castle**, a country mansion almost cut off by water. At **Lenham** the worst of the climb has been surmounted. To the left little lanes rise to the most attractive piece of upland in East Kent, particularly noteworthy at Longbeech Wood.

Charing is an old centre at an important crossroad. Its antiquity is typified by the remains of the archbishop's palace near the church. Both Lenham and Charing are by passed, but both should be visited. Beyond Hotfield Common the road gains **Ashford**, a railway centre.

The next section runs through quieter country by Smeeth to **Hythe**, a Cinque Port, now set back from the sea, with an old church containing a collection of human bones, thus rivalling the impressive set at Rothwell, in Northants. At Seabrook and Sandgate the coast is reached and it is then only a short journey into **Folkestone** by the upper road.

TO CANTERBURY, DOVER AND THE ISLE OF THANET

From London Bridge, by the Old Kent Road to New Cross Gate as on page 104, and then by Lewisham to beyond Lee Green. Instead of going right for Sidcup, however, the road through Eltham (A210) should be used by Blackfen to Dartford Heath and the Dartford by-pass. This is less congested than the old route by Shooters Hill, Welling and Dartford.

The Dover Road is not of great interest until beyond Rochester. It follows the modernized line of the Roman Watling Street. North of Rochester, on the edge of the Thames, are the Cooling Marshes, identified with the hair-raising scenes in the opening of "Great Expectations". At Cobham, south of the main road, stands the Leather Bottle Inn, another Dickens relic. Rochester and Chatham have both plenty of touring interest, but the greatest single historical attraction is Canterbury, 55 miles from London. Here the road divides: Watling Street turns more towards the south-east for Dover, another and quieter, highway keeps straight on for Sandwich, touching the fringe of the colliery district, and a further road bends towards the north-east for Margate, Ramsgate and North Foreland.

The Kent colliery workings in a limited part of the area enclosed by the Canterbury-Margate-Dover triangle, do not intrude upon the landscape like those in the older pit districts. Modern plant, sound planning and a social conscience have all contributed to a happier state of affairs.

There are few possibilities of avoiding the main road until after Rochester because of the scarcity of bridges across the River Medway. Beyond Rochester, however, a number of lane routes are available. The whole line of A2 as far as Rochester is busy on week-days and at holiday times. The best way to Dover, therefore, is probably through Lenham and Ashford, using one or other of the alternatives suggested on previous pages.

From the east end of the Dartford by-pass, the main road continues nearly straight, leaving Gravesend to the left. Beyond Northumberland Bottom the road rises and the estuary of the Thames can be seen beyond the smoke of Gravesend. The highway remains fairly solitary and without great interest until it begins to dip into the Medway Valley. Ahead there is a notable view of Rochester.

Through Strood, the western suburb of Rochester, the bridge across the Medway is taken into Rochester.

Rochester, with its allied towns of Chatham and Gillingham, are so close to each other that they are often called "The Medway Towns". The river broadens here and flows swiftly towards the sea. The site of Rochester Castle was used by the Britons. The nineteenth-century Rochester was well-known to Dickens. The town still contains several old houses. It is the castle which dominates the town, however, and its great square keep is a landmark for many miles around. Until the reign of Edward IV the castle was in good condition and was for long regarded as impregnable. It is now owned by the town. The small Early English and Norman cathedral is close to the castle. Adjoining **Chatham** is best known for its Royal Dockyard.

Gad's Hill, three miles north-west of Rochester, on the Gravesend Road, has an old inn, the Sir John Falstaff, reputed to be on the site of the place where Sir John met the "Men in buckram", in *Henry IV*. Dickens lived at Gad's Hill Place, near the inn, from

1857 to 1870. The marshes north of Rochester are threaded by several by-roads but it is not easy to get close to the Thames and Medway estuaries. An exception is the Medwayside resort of Upnor, quite close to Rochester, on the west side.

From Chatham, A2 rises to a ridge and keeps a ruler-like course for Canterbury, passing an unfinished temple very soon. This is a fruit-growing district, at its best in blossom time. The first town is **Sittingbourne**, an industrial centre, and beyond it attractive lanes go tight to the downs and left to the levels of The Swale.

An alternative route along lanes runs north of the main road between Rochester and Sittingbourne and on to Faversham and Dunkirk. It first leads through Gillingham, the largest borough in Kent, and then by Lower Rainham and Upchurch to Milton and Sittingbourne, keeping close to the flats near the mouth of the River Medway. This by-lane route may be continued past Sittingbourne by going left at Snipeshill, west of Sittingbourne, and continuing close to the railway by Teynham Station and through Davington and **Faversham**, a quiet place with a large church, to Dunkirk, about five miles west of Canterbury.

After Sittingbourne A2 traverses a pleasant tract of country by Ospringe, passes Faversham and then comes into a picturesque belt of wooded land. On Boughton Hill there is a fine view westward towards Faversham. Past Dunkirk the straight road reaches Harbledown, from which there is a further splendid prospect, this time across the valley of the River Stout at Canterbury.

Canterbury, described in full on pages 135–136, lies in peaceful country. After a right turn on entering the town, the Dover Road goes tight through, in a south-easterly direction. This section of the road, partly over high ground, is also straight but has plenty of interest. The Downs south of Canterbury are spacious, well served by roads and deserve close exploration. Their valleys are often secluded and delightful.

After a stretch of open country the road dips to Bridge, attractively situated on the Little Stour River, and then begins to mount Barham Downs. There are good views on both sides, especially at Lydden Hill.

Lydden lies in a hollow and the final stretch into Dover runs along a narrow valley, For Dover, see pages 133–134.

TO MARGATE AND RAMSGATE

From Canterbury the route lies along A28 through Sturry. Fordwich, on the right, was the port of Canterbury when the Isle of Thanet was really an island. The Caen stone for Canterbury Cathedral came this way. At Sarre the road divides. The main road continues across the marshland past St. Nicolas-at-Wade and by Birchington and Westgate-on-Sea to **Margate** (see page 137).

At Sarre, the Ramsgate road goes rightward. After 1½ miles, however, it is worthwhile using the loop road to the south which leads by Monkton to Minster-in-Thanet, which has a fine Early English and Norman church, and so into Ramsgate (see page 137).

Cycling between London and the South Coast today

As Harold Briercliffe wrote this cycle route guide in the late 1940s, many of the roads he mentions are now busier than they were and are not suitable for cycling today. Suggested alternative cycle routes, from Sustrans, which are in the same location as Harold's original route are listed below. To devise your own detailed route and map in the region, go to www.sustrans.org.uk/map for online mapping, and free iphone and android cycling apps.

The Cuckoo Trail is an incredibly popular 10-mile traffic-free converted railway path running from **Polegate** to **Heathfield**. This route is part of **National Cycle Network Route 21**, which runs all the way from **London** to **Eastbourne** via **Crawley**, **East Grinstead**, **Eridge**, **Heathfield** and **Polegate**. This route provides a combination of traffic-free paths and sections on minor roads. The trail runs through a mixture of broadleaf woodland, open grassland, arable farmland and pasture.

National Route 20 runs from **Wandsworth** on the River Thames, straight down to **Brighton** via **Redhill** and **Crawley**. This route is roughly 57 miles and combines traffic-free sections with sections on minor roads but also features a gap between Woodmansterne and north of Redhill.

The **Downs Link Route** is one of the longest converted railway path cycle routes in the country. The quality of the surface is variable but it still provides an enjoyable route that runs for around 35 miles from **Guildford** down to **Hove** pretty much entirely traffic free.

Useful maps and books (available from www.sustransshop.co.uk): *Kent and East Sussex Cycle Tours; Surrey and West Sussex Cycle Tours; Kent: Cycling Country Lanes (Goldeneye Cycling Guides); Sussex and South Surrey Goldeneye Cycling map;* and *Explore Kent by Bike.*

The inside story

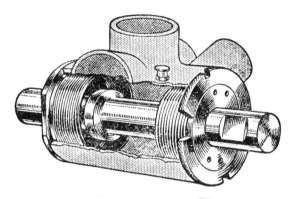

on easy cycling

CHAPTER V

THE SOUTH COAST

THE conventional reply by a seasoned (and cynical) tourist to the query "What is there in cycling along the south coast?" is "Nothing!" This is an over-simplification which evades reality.

I will try to make myself clear. It is true that cycle touring between Portsmouth and Ramsgate can be a trying journey through a string of crowded holiday resorts. It is true that nearly everywhere where a road runs down to the sea there are likely to be other people. It is true that the larger resorts do not cater for the passing cyclist, preferring (naturally enough) the holiday maker who stays for a week or more.

When all that has been said, the worst has been spoken. Actually, there are stretches of coastline which have not been over-built. Perhaps the worst piece for building is that between Selsey Bill and Seaford. There are other bad patches to the east, Bexhill to Hastings, neat Winchelsea (once quiet and unspoilt) and at odd places to the north-east, between Whitstable and Herne Bay for instance.

The wise tourist will keep away from these belts of London on-Sea, ride a little way inland on the by-roads and only dip down to the coast now and then. Certain places on the coast he ought to visit: Bosham, Littlehampton, Beachy Head (the finest bit of coastal scenery in the South of England), Folkestone, Dover.

Inland in Sussex and Kent there is a great deal to interest the tourist. West Sussex has wooded ridges (about Goodwood, for instance) that are as lovely as any in the country. The South Downs are the boldest manifestations of chalk in England. The Weald, lying between the North Downs and the South Downs, is a fascinating belt for the explorer: a district full of charm, with old houses, castles, forest-land and rivers.

Kent is one of the most varied of the long-settled counties of England. In Saxon and Norman days its civilisation was higher than that of the areas to the west and north-west. Its position on the main highways to the Continent from London kept it in the forefront of culture.

In these days the area enclosed within the lines London-Farnham-Maidstone-Rochester-Gravesend-London are largely suburbanized and, as such, do not come within the main purview of this guide.

The tour which follows commences at Portsmouth because many people who have toured the Isle of Wight cross to Portsmouth and continue along the South Coast. Anyone coming from farther west, however, from Dorset and the New Forest, could join in at Havant. Similarly, the tourist who follows the Portsmouth Road from London could also join in at Havant without going into Portsmouth.

To end (or start) arguments, I would like to state here that "Kentish Men" live west of the River Medway and that "Men of Kent" dwell east of it.

Tourist accommodation along the south coast and even inland is not so plentiful as in some parts of the country. However, bed and breakfast can generally be obtained in the larger inland villages, while the towns are usually reliable enough for accommodation (some of it rather expensive). Suitable halting places are indicated in the text.

Youth hostels are not by any means so frequent as in the west and north. The only ones suitable for the tourist travelling parallel to the coast, or more or less along it, are at Arundel, Patcham, Blackboys (near Uckfield), High Halden, Dover and Canterbury. Those approaching Kent from the north by the Tilbury-Gravesend ferry will find that the hostel at Puckeridge west of Bishop's Stortford (in Hertfordshire) is a useful halt.

Nearly all the coast towns have their "official" camp sites. The practised camper will, however, prefer to find the less sophisticated sites lying farther inland. The sites list (members only) of the Camping Club of Great Britain contains many desirable camp sites in the southern counties.

One more reason for starting this tour from the west is that the prevailing wind comes from that direction.

APPROACHES

The main road approaches to the South Coast are fully described in chapter 4 (pages 89–109). Portsmouth can be approached also from the north through Oxford, Newbury, Whitchurch and Winchester. Oxford is readily reached from Birmingham, Manchester and the West Riding towns.

There is an excellent railway service between Waterloo and Portsmouth, and also between Waterloo and Arundel or Chichester for those starting east of Portsmouth. Still farther east, Brighton and Lewes are also approached by fast electric services.

In using the railway to the south coast from London, it is as well to remember that most of the early evening trains are crowded with business people. It is therefore best to travel before 4 p.m. Similarly, return trains to London are busiest in the morning. Going back to London, the afternoon trains are to be preferred.

Visitors from the northern and midland counties approaching Kent first (instead of reaching it last as in the tour which follows) have a useful way of getting there without touching London. This is to make first for Bishop's Stortford, and then to travel by Hatfield Heath, Chipping Ongar, and Brentwood to Tilbury. At Tilbury there is a regular ferry across to Gravesend, for Rochester.

Another unorthodox way of reaching North Kent (Margate or Ramsgate) is to travel by the "Golden Eagle" steamers from Tower Bridge, London. Bicycles can be taken on the steamers, which ply only in the summer months. The steamers are also useful for the return journey.

The tour which follows is based on the assumption that the tourist starts at Portsmouth (or Havant) and returns from Margate (or Gravesend).

Useful through trains now run every week-day morning from Newcastle, Sheffield and Nottingham to Winchester (for Portsmouth) and on Saturday afternoons only between Ramsgate, Margate and Herne Bay to Nottingham and Sheffield.

The point-to-point vouchers issued by the cycling bodies and the Y.H.A. are very useful for the tour which follows: out to Portsmouth (or Winchester) and back from Ramsgate (or Margate).

TOUR OF THE SOUTHERN COUNTIES
From Portsmouth to Gravesend—256 miles

Leave Portsmouth (Harbour) by way of The Hard, Queen Street, Edinburgh Road, and Commercial Road. (Look out, on the left, for the birthplace of Dickens, at No. 393 Commercial Road, now equipped as a museum. Dickens was born there in 1812).

The road leads across Portsbridge Creek into Cosham. Where the main London Road (A3) keeps straight ahead, turn rightward for **Havant** (eight miles from Portsmouth), a small town.

From Havant a bridge leads over to **Hayling Island**, a low-lying island and resort to the south.

The road eastward remains suburbanized as far as **Emsworth**, beyond which it enters Sussex. Lanes run northward to the inviting district of Stansted Forest. Over the low land to the right the Isle of Wight can be seen. Several water channels leading southward across the meadows are crossed and then, near Bosham Station, a lane runs rightward into Bosham, (15) a fishing village partly preserved by the National Trust. The place has plenty of interest, including a small church dating from the time of Edward the Confessor. Bosham has been connected with the story of Canute and the waves.

Other lanes lead back to the main road, a little east of the approach road, and there follows more flat going (enlivened a little at New Fishbourne by the head of the Chichester Channel) until the Chichester by-pass strikes rightward. The tourist should go straight ahead into Chichester.

Chichester, (19) a bright cathedral town, is of Roman origin, as its centre, where four roads meet, denotes. The market cross is an ornate structure dating from about A.D. 1500. The cathedral visible over a wide radius—even out to sea—built in Norman style, was begun in A.D. 1090 and in its early years had many additions. More recently, it has been restored. Its bell tower is 120 ft. high and may be climbed.

From Chichester the main road eastward (A27) should be followed through a varied countryside. The roadside views are pleasant rather than striking.

About six miles from Chichester it is possible to fork leftward along A29 and then turn left into **Slindon**, a delightful village set on a hillside. To the west stretches Slindon Park, full of fine beeches. Northwards smooth chalk valleys sidle up towards the tree-crowned ridges.

A dense belt of woodland has to be crossed before the fall into Arundel, which is entered by a narrow street.

Arundel (30) is a mediaeval survival into the twentieth century. The castle completely overawes the town—Arundel Castle might be said to be Arundel. The castle site is a superb one, on a knoll overlooking the marshes of the River Arun at a bridge. The river here pierces the South Downs and the site of the castle must have been of great strategic advantage in feudal times. The castle is now used by the Duke of Norfolk and not generally shown to visitors. Much of the park can be visited, however.

Arundel is suggested as a halting place for two nights. There is bed and breakfast accommodation in the town, while there is also a youth hostel at Warningcamp, about 2½ miles away, reached by a lane going north-east from near Arundel Station, which is on A27, a little south-east of the river bridge.

The most attractive short evening run from Arundel is to Littlehampton, four miles southward. The route is past the station and then rightward through Lyminster to the mouth of the Arun at **Littlehampton**. The resort is relatively small and quiet and has river as well as beach charm. There are good sands and excellent bathing.

Return to Arundel for the night (38).

A full day's run towards the north from Arundel brings in the lovely course of the River Arun and its tributary the River Rother, besides splendid views of the South Downs and visits to several villages of great historic and intrinsic interest.

From Arundel, the road going north-eastward from the north side of the bridge should be followed into Arundel Park. Here the castle rises in its magnificence to the left but of equal interest is the fine avenue along which the road goes to Swansbourne Lake, a sinuous sheet seen in a hollow to the left. The path on the north-east side of the lake should be followed afoot for some way.

The by-road next curves round the foot of the park, keeping to low ground, and reaches the river again at a small quarry. There is a fork here, at which the way is leftward through a wooded cutting, but there is recompense in leaving the bicycle again, briefly, and walking past a riverside inn, with tables under the trees, to the boats some way ahead, and then looking back at the prospect over the meadows and the curving river at the pile of Arundel Castle rising against the sky and the ridge climbing rightward away from the roofs. This is one of the most notable riverside views in the South of England.

The Arun, near Amberley

The route passes through the cutting to the left and then undulates sharply to the neat village of South Stoke which is almost surrounded by the Arun. A bridge leads over into the water meadows on the east side of the stream. The way ahead is barred—as a notice indicates—but the path alongside the river, going leftward, leads along through willows to a footbridge at the foot of a meadow, up which a track strikes northward into North Stoke. From North Stoke a by-lane goes northward with the railway to Amberley Station. This is fishermen's country, and there is a cosy inn nearby.

For Amberley, see page 120.

The next stage is to cross the Arun again into Houghton, where a right turn leads northward into **Bury**, (43) an old and attractive village amongst the water meadows by the river. To the south-east, Rackham Hill raises a bold head. Downland Sussex looks at its best hereabouts. To the west Bignor Hill forms another bastion of the Downs.

At the south end of Bury a by-lane runs eastward and across the main road (Arundel-Pulborough) to travel under the graceful slopes of the Downs past West Burton into **Bignor**. Here are the remains of a Roman Villa. Tessellated pavements are on view on certain days of the week. The lane continues into Sutton, giving fine views of the Downs to the left. The route keeps to the hillfoot past Barlavington and emerges on the Chichester-Petworth road at the foot of Duncton Hill (see page 93).

Duncton village (48) is mostly crammed along the road edges. Beyond it, going north, the highway climbs over a hill and begins to drop towards Petworth. The recommended route, however, strikes rightward less than half a mile south of Petworth Station and immediately becomes a secluded lane running through parkland. One mile farther south-east it reaches the north bank of a large lake in Burton Park. This reedy sheet fills a choice hollow and beyond it rise the tree-covered ridges. This is a cool corner on the warmest day and is perhaps the most charming of the accessible lakes—such few as there are—in Sussex. Afterwards the lane goes through a heathy wilderness, full of ancient evergreens and peacefulness. Tiny Coates village marks a return to more ordinary landscapes and soon there is a left turn down to Fittleworth Station and bridge. The bridge crosses the Rother at a spot beloved by fishermen and just beyond there is an ivyed inn with a signboard hanging across the road.

A right turn and then another lead through a corner of Fittleworth village and to A283, which first climbs steeply and then descends more gradually to Stopham Bridge.

Stopham Bridge, for all its traffic lights, is one of the finest bridges in Britain. It is narrow and has jutting piers and a high central arch for navigation which puts it, almost, into a class of its own.

From the bridge it is a short run into **Pulborough** (56), which is described on page 95. The run back to Arundel by Whiteways Lodge is described on the same page.

Arundel, second time (64).

The next part of the tour brings the cyclist closer to the Downs and offers the "rough-stuff" rider an alternative which introduces two historic sites in Chanctonbury Ring and Cissbury Ring.

STOPHAM BRIDGE.

From Arundel the way leads back to Whiteways Lodge, there going rightward for Houghton and Amberley Station. Just north of Amberley Station, the gateway of Amberley Castle can be seen ahead. The road leading towards it is private, however, so that the tourist must keep on the lane curving rightward at the foot of the downs. Soon, however, a signpost points leftward to **Amberley** (69), an old and compact village which in recent years has had a modern housing estate tacked on to the east side of it without in any way impairing the character of the old village. The winding village street leads westward to the flint-built Norman church but a gate between the churchyard and the castle bars a nearer approach to the latter. However, by dropping down a short hill to the marshes, the bold, tall north wall of the castle can be seen splendidly as it looks across the flat meadows stretching northward.

The road along the foothills of the downs undulated eastward by Springhead Farm—a cosy nook north of the road and into **Storrington** (73), an old village on the scenic greensand formation. The village is now modernized and enlarged, but the beauty of its situation remains.

The run remains full of incident as it makes for Washington. On the right the slopes of the downs remain suave: their summits treeless. A landmark at their feet is Sullington Church, perched on a jutting shoulder.

Washington (76) lies on the main Worthing road (see page 95) but nevertheless retains much of its charm. The route goes rightward towards Worthing and then leaves the main highway as it turns eastward again. Prominent on the bare downs to the right now is **Chanctonbury Ring**, the most famous landmark in Sussex. The Ring is a thick plantation perched on the edge of the bare downs. It is a feature of the views of the downs from the Weald south of Billingshurst, Horsham and Cowfold.

About 1½ miles east of Washington there is a crossroads. Through the trees which line the road Chanctonbury Ring appears at its most arresting.

———————————

A rough-stuff alternative to the main route commences at this crossroads. The alternative includes the ascent to Chanctonbury Ring and a continuation across the downs to Cissbury Ring and the outskirts of Worthing. The hardest part is the mile-long push to the ridge. Thereafter the upland tracks are rough but mostly passable in the saddle.

From the crossroads the Chanctonbury lane strikes southward. For a few hundred yards it can be ridden but at a gate leading into a grove to the right the lane becomes a chalky track which ascends in two very sharp bends to the side of a plantation—now being regrettably thinned—which reaches up the steep shanks of hill to Chanctonbury Ring.

It is a hard push up the sunken trackway to the ridge some way east of the Ring and beside the upper fringe of the hillside plantation.

The through route goes straight ahead, southward, as a grassy track. Another track strikes westward towards Chanctonbury Ring, which is a long half-mile to the west. This westward-going track is bumpy and rises sharply near the Ring, close to which the bicycle can be left.

On close examination the Ring is found to be a knoll overlooking the Weald. It has ancient entrenchment, around its sides and some modern ones, too—emplacements and trenches of the 1939-45 war. The chief feature, however, is the grove of sobbing beeches—there is always a wind at Chanctonbury's altitude of 783 ft. above sea level. The trees were planted about the middle of the eighteenth century by a local landowner. Nowadays many of them are uprooted and ailing, but sufficient remain to make the most outstanding landmark for miles.

The through route strikes southward and is quite smooth riding for some time as the edges of dwarf plantations are passed. Then it descends to a gate, where the way is straight ahead across another trackway. Soon the through route begins to curve leftward and climbs the east side of Cissbury Ring.

Cissbury Ring, which is 603 ft. above sea level, is now the property of the National Trust. It occupies the crown of a large hilltop and has a deep entrenchment. The hill forms the largest British camp on the South Downs. One theory holds that it was the "factory" of a great flint-mining area.

From the eastern edge of Cissbury the track dips down sharply to the east side of a golf course and for a while the going is bumpy. It improves, however, and when the first Worthing villas are met at Charman Dean there are metalled roads once more.

From the signpost below Chanctonbury Ring to Charman Dean the total distance is about six miles. With sightseeing, the journey deserves two full hours.

There is no need to enter Worthing, which can be skirted on the east side. The main road runs eastward past Lancing to the wooden bridge at Old Shoreham. It is perhaps profitably, however, to go through Broadwater and to the shore road well east of Worthing.

The next three miles along the coast road, by South Lancing to the new bridge at Shoreham, ate likely to act as a corrective to any thoughts of following the coastline closely. Traffic is heavy, the building is most indiscriminate, and the waste land, when it appears, is really and truly waste. It is a relief to cross the bridge into Shoreham and turn leftward by Old Shoreham up the valley of the River Adur. The conspicuous modern chapel of Lancing College to the left does not improve the view, but the valley of the Adur, between soothing chalk slopes, is some compensation, except where a huge quarry intrudes.

Upper Beeding and Bramber, pleasing villages on opposite sides of the river make fitting preliminaries to **Steyning**, an old borough, recommended as a halting place. The total distance of this (partly) "rough-stuff" loop is about 17 miles.

From the crossroads north of Chanctonbury Ring the main route performs a graceful curve, with fine views on the right of the bare ramparts of the downs, and next runs into **Steyning** (80).

Steyning is one of the most attractive of the little towns which lie inland from the busy resorts of the south coast. Inevitably it shares in some of their popularity, but in the off-season and in the evening, Steyning resumes its rightful place as an old borough. There is plenty of quaint architecture in the streets of the town and the general impression is of antiquity and peace. At the time of the Domesday Book, Steyning was one of the largest cities in England. St. Andrew's Church dates back to Henry I and has an ornamented nave. Steyning or the nearby villages of Bramber and Beeding are recommended as halting places.

From Steyning it is an easy downland walk of six miles return to Chanctonbury Ring (see page 121.) The walk can be shortened by descending direct from the Ring to the crossroads cast of Washington (see page 121) from which a 'bus service runs into Steyning.

An obvious evening excursion from Steyning, either by bicycle, train or 'bus, is to Brighton, some 11 miles south-east and reached through Shoreham and Portslade.

Brighton, the largest seaside resort in Britain and also a residential "suburb" of London is too big a subject for a book on cycle-touring. It dates from the Domesday Book and until the middle of the eighteenth century was a fishing village. It has a seafront four miles long and most of the conventional attractions for the holidaymaker.

On from Steyning the through route makes for Bramber with its shell of a castle and its old church perched up on the left, and over the Adur into Beeding.

Here a side-road goes leftward and trails round the northern feet of the downs through a set of three villages dating back to Saxon times: Edburton, Fulking and Poynings. Edburton is essentially a tiny place grouped around a tree-shrouded Early English church. Fulking is a little way farther on. Larger than either is **Poynings**, which has an unusual church. A little way southward, and worth the exertion of the walk, is the **Devil's Dyke**, a deep narrow hollow. To the south of the dyke rises a hill from which there is a good view of Brighton to the south and of the Weald to the north.

The road goes north and then east again as it skirts the picturesque flanks of Newtimber Hill. Then it joins the main Brighton road (A23) and follows this past Pyecombe after which it swings left off the main highway towards Clayton to the north.

Three miles south of the junction with the road for Clayton is Patcham, which lies east of the new by-pass, leaving it in peace. At Patcham there is a youth hostel, lying to the north-west side of the village and close to the northern end of the by-pass. The hostel has room for 80. It is recommended as an alternative to Steyning.

On the hills to the north-east of Patcham stands the Indian Chattri Memorial to Hindu and Sikh soldiers who died in Brighton as a result of service in the 1914-18 war. The memorial is eight-sided and stands high on the downs.

The through route after turning left off the Brighton Road runs parallel with the Clayton Tunnel into **Clayton** (92). On the downs to the right are Jack and Jill, windmills which are great landmarks. A right turn at the church in Clayton continues the downfoot route to the east.

The downs rise in characteristic folds and crests on the right until, nearing Westmeston, they lift to **Ditchling Beacon**, the highest point in this part of the South Downs (853 ft.) The road continues to wind towards the east, follow ing a profile cunningly traced along the northern slopes.

Near Offham the East Grinstead-Lewes main road is met and thereafter the immediate objective is Lewes, which rises on a strategic ridge towards the south-east and above the deep valley of the River Ouse.

Lewes (101) was the ancient capital of Sussex and remains one of the most distinctive towns in Britain. It is dominated by a Norman-Plantagenet castle, which is approached through bold gateways to the north of the High Street. Lewes makes a good headquarters for walks over the downs to the west and east. The former youth hostel is not available at the time of writing (June, 1949).

The next part of the route draws nearer to the coast and introduces the tourist to Beachy Head. From Lewes the route first drops steeply down and crosses the bridge across the Ouse to the east side of the river. Here the way is rightward through less interesting scenes than those met before Lewes. On the left, however, rises the smoothly moulded shape of Mount Caburn. A lane turns leftward off the main route into Glynde. At Glyndebourne House, a little northward, musical and dramatic festivals are held.

In the village of Beddingham and on the low levels of the Ouse the route turns rightward, leaving the main road to Eastbourne (see page 128). Beddingham Church, to the right, has a picturesque setting. The lane followed keeps to the low ground through country which is not particularly inviting. Ahead the derricks and warehouses of Newhaven, near the side of the river, can be seen. The route keeps to the east bank and instead of crossing the bridge into Newhaven keeps leftward for Bishopstone, where the new station straddles the road.

The coast road into Seaford reaches a gap turn by the sea into the land defences. On the beach there is a Martello Tower, built as a precaution against a Napoleonic invasion.

There is no roadway ahead close to the coast, which begins to assume a more promising contour. Side roads strike northward and eastward through Seaford, a small and well-planned resort with many private schools, to the main "coast" road, A259. At a hilltop crossroads 1½ miles east of Seaford there is a striking transformation in the outlook. The villas and schools seem to disappear in an instant as the road tips into the Cuckmere Valley.

The Cuckmere Valley
Sussex.

The Cuckmere Valley, some of which is preserved (fortunately) by the National Trust, is a deep trench extending between the downs and taking the winding Cuckmere River. Although the main road crosses it and there are secondary roads towards the north along the riverside, the valley and the hills rising to the northward wear a wild look. In winter the tourist looking for the first time at the scene might be excused for thinking himself transported to the remoter parts of the Craven Highlands, in West Yorkshire.

The highway descends fairly sharply to the bridge at Exceat, a farmsteading tucked in the lee of a hill. To the south footpaths run to Cuckmere Haven, 1½ miles away. From the haven, there is a fine view eastward along the coast at the **Seven Sisters**, the cliffs west of Beachy Head. Northward from Exceat a road runs by Litlington to Lullington, which has one of the smallest churches in England. On the west side of the river is **Alfriston**, a compact village with a fine church, a timber-built parsonage and the shaft of a market cross. Closer to Exceat, tucked away in a valley to the north-east, is picturesque West Dean.

From Exceat the highway rises sharply to a ridge. Over the forestry plantations on the left West Dean village can be seen laid out in all its neatness. The plantations persist all the way up the two-mile rise to Friston, a crossroads village closely pressed by a modern housing estate to the north-east.

South and south-west from Friston extends the large stretch of downland and cliff known as the Crowlink Estate, a possession of the National Trust. Signboards indicate that vehicles are prohibited, but it is usually permissible to wheel a bicycle over the open downland by Went Hill and to join a coastwise track which emerges at Birling Gap. From the high ground west of Birling Gap it is possible, from the cliff edge, to look across at the saw-tooth form of the Seven Sisters to the west.

At East Dean, a naturally attractive village east of Friston, a side-lane bears rightward and descends by Birling Farm to the coast at Birling Gap, where there is a coastguard station and also facilities for meals. The cliffs are low at **Birling Gap** and from the beach the Seven Sisters to the west, and the cliffs rising towards Beachy Head in the east, form splendid pictures. I would add that in summer Birling Gap is very popular with family motoring parties.

From Birling Gap, a road turns inland over the open pastures on the landward side of Beachy Head. From the virtual sea level at Birling Gap, this road climbs steadily, passing at one point an old sighing plantation on the right which reminds the observant rider once again of the similarity between the chalk and limestone geological formations.

About 4 miles east of Birling Gap the road reaches the sea again, this time on a ledge of green turf between the summit of the cliff called Belle Tout (284 ft.) and Beachy Head. On Belle Tout there are the remains of an old lighthouse. It is possible here to peer over the cliffs at the beach 150 ft. below. Eastward the lip of the cliff rises steadily to Beachy Head. The lighthouse, a little out from the base of the cliff can be seen.

The road next climbs consistently for 1½ miles up a shallow upland valley to the summit of Beachy Head, near the coastguard station and some war-time erections.

Beachy Head, 575 ft. high, is without doubt the most outstanding natural feature of the south coast. It is the grandest chalk cliff in Britain. From the unfenced crest of the land—the edge should not be approached too closely as there are frequent landslips—the cliff falls almost vertically to the rocky beach, on which the lighthouse is dwarfed by the immensity of the Head.

On the next stretch of road Eastbourne spreads out below like a map. There is a choice of descents into the town from the road from Beachy Head.

Eastbourne (126) is recommended as a halting place for the night. There is no youth hostel nearby, but there are alternative, and quieter, halting places inland, to the north.

Eastbourne is a large resort catering for all holidaymaking tastes, It has a fine three-level esplanade and makes much of its proximity, by skilful publicity, to Beachy Head and the scenery of inland Sussex.

Between **Beddingham** and Polegate (for Eastbourne) the main road A274) skirts the north side of the downs. Across Firle Park the downs rise to **Firle Beacon** (718 ft.) the summit of a narrow ridge, which remains a feature of the southward view until Berwick is reached. Then across the flats of the Cuckmere Valley the **Long Man of Wilmington** comes into view. The Long Man is a figure 240 ft. tall cut in the chalk and, like most hillside figures, probably originated as a pagan fertility symbol. From Berwick, Wilmington and Polegate, lateral lanes run southward to the Seaford-Eastbourne road. At Polegate the Eastbourne road strikes off A247 and leads into the resort by Willingdon. Lewes-Eastbourne by this route, 17 miles.

The continuation of the tour eastwards from Eastbourne (or Polegate) heads first of all for **Pevensey** (131). Pevensey and adjoining Westham, for all their main-road position, are full of visible history. In Westham, which is reached first, there is an old house with a projecting upper storey and also a dignified church. Pevensey's greatest feature is the castle, once on an island. There is a bold west gate, with evidence of a drawbridge, while the modern road trails round the north side of the outer wall which bulges with nine solid bastions.

Beyond the bridge at the east end of Pevensey, a road goes leftward off the main road and out to the quiet Pevensey Levels. A right turn shortly afterwards takes the rider over rich marshland towards the line of the old cliff. A climb up a sunken depression leads into **Wartling**, a tiny and very harmoniously-grouped village. To the north-west lies Herstmonceux Castle, now an observatory. A right turn in Wartling gives access to an undulating lane which emerges on a ridge at the main-road village of Boreham Street, where a friendly welcome, meals and overnight accommodation may be had at the Chestnut Tree Cottage, which is kept by two club cyclists, Mr. and Mrs. King.

Next, the route, keeping well inland and off the more frequented routes, tips into a valley, in which a lane leads off to the left to climb to a long tongue of land from which there are fine views across Ashburnham Park.

This lane route soon reaches **Battle** (see page 103). The next stretch of road runs over high ground along A21, leaving the site of the Battle of Hastings on the right, and then drops into Hastings.

Hastings (549) is one of the most distinctive resorts on the south coast. Its situation, at the limit of a sand ridge, gives the cliffs their red and orange hues. There is a three-mile front and conventional seaside amusements. William I, who landed between Pevensey and Hastings, used the town as a base, and the castle was built soon after the Norman Conquest. The walk eastward from Hastings along the cliffs to Fairlight Glen is one of the most striking coastal trips in East Sussex.

The direct road between Pevensey and Hastings travels across the featureless levels and, on higher ground, by-passes the smart resort of Bexhill-on-Sea before reaching Hastings through St. Leonards—a total distance of 14 miles.

The tourist who has reached Hastings and must curtail his holiday could, en route for London or Guildford, travel along one of the finest high-level routes in Sussex. This runs from Battle north-westward by Netherfield Road to a lonely hill-top church, where the direction lies leftward along a quiet ridge road. There is rich woodland on this route and peeps into lovely parks. The route is at its best in and near the hollow known as Darwell Hole. Farther on, a side-road leads rightward to **Brightling Beacon**, a splendid viewpoint 647 ft. above sea level.

The Needle at Brightling Beacon was erected by Jack Fuller, an eccentric squire who died in 1834. From it, on a clear day, the coast of France can be seen. Near Woods Corner, in a field on the north side of the Battle-Heathfield ridge road which is followed by this route, stands another of his works, a sugar-loaf erection, hollow within and about 25 ft. high. The sugar-loaf looks like a candle-extinguisher and is alleged to be linked with a bet made by Fuller.

The ridge road continues, after a steep drop and rise, into more populated regions. This is an area of independent smallholders, living on the southern slope of the ridge and enjoying many hours of sunshine in every year. At Cade Street, on the north side of the road, is a pillar commemorating Jack Cade, the fifteenth-century peasant leader whose only mistake was that he was well ahead of his time: most of his demands would seem quite moderate today.

At the large village of **Heathfield** there is a railway station and a resident colony of people who work in London and live in this pleasant place. West of Heathfield stands the road junction of Cross-in-Hand and from it highways go to Eastbourne; London and Lewes. A little farther west, in a good woodland situation, is the youth hostel of **Blackboys**, a useful halting place.

An undulating and not unpicturesque road continues the main route from Hastings, first over the hill beyond the north-easterly suburb of Ore and by Copshall and Icklesham into Winchelsea.

Winchelsea (158) itself, and not the newer growths nearer the coast, is a fascinating old town on a promontory to the south side of the River Brede. It dates back to Saxon days, but its town-plan owes its origin to a dispensation of Edward I. In a central square stands a fine church in the Early English Decorated style built of Caen stone.

The Land and New Gates of the town are other notable features.

Three miles of easy going, much of it along the riverside, lead into Rye.

Rye (161) is recommended as a place for overnight accommodation. Its red roofs rise from the levels in a pile which has its apex at the church. Rye stands on a table of dark sandstone and from its church tower there is a fine view, taking in the meeting of the Brede and the Rother at their mouth and also the remains of Camber Castle on the marshes to the south. Ypres Tower and the Land Gate are other historical features of Rye.

From Rye the recommended route keeps inland (see below for an alternative). First it goes northward by Iden and into Kent to The Stocks, on the Isle of Oxney (once actually an island), where the way is rightwards to lower ground at Stone. Picturesque Appledore is kept to the right as the highway runs on firm ground, with an area of woodland charm on the left. The tree-lined Royal Military Canal, on the right, marks a former border between land and sea and was cut between 1804 and 1806 as a defensive measure against Napoleon. It runs from Rye to Hythe, thus enclosing Romney Marsh.

From hereabouts Kentish oast-houses, with their candle snuffer heads, begin to get more frequent. Through a quiet countryside the route keeps to the landward side of the Royal Military Canal, passing through Warehorne, Huckinge and Bonnington before climbing to higher ground. Thence by **Lympne**, with its airport and impressive views southward across Romney Marsh, and so into Hythe.

Hythe (187) is a silted-up port, now a resort. The church on its hilltop, is well buttressed and on different levels. The town has rambling streets and old houses.

The alternative runs along the coast and across Romney Marsh from Rye to Hythe and is attractive because of the strangeness of the marshland: its long horizons, clouds and sheep. In places the beaches are marred by huts and other temporary dwellings and by relics of the 1939-45 war.

For about two miles this route follows the main road for New Romney, but at the far end of the house-lined avenue comes to East Guldeford Church, an ancient edifice in Tudor brickwork. By turning right here a lane can be followed to Camber. From this lane there is a good view of Rye. Camber is a modern growth, but beyond it the road keeps along the sea wall and there are pleasant outlooks over the marshes and dikes at the farmsteads inland. Farther on, the lane goes inland towards Lydd.

Lydd wears a pleasing appearance as it is approached from the marsh, largely because of the elms, but closer acquaintance shows that it suffers by being at the gates of a large military camp.

South-eastward from Lydd a lane runs to Dungeness in about four miles. The route is a monotonous one and the black-banded lighthouse seems to get nearer very slowly. "The Pilot" inn has a modern appearance, but is very old inside, with a saloon bar which has a ceiling built from the timbers of a Spanish vessel wrecked on the coast. Lunches and teas are available. The tall lighthouse looks across at that on Cap Gris-Nez, in France, some 20 miles away. "Pluto", the pipeline to France in the invasion by British forces, had its English end here. The eight-mile return journey from Lydd to **Dungeness** and back is not accounted in the general mileage of the tour.

From Lydd, the alternative route strikes north-west to **New Romney**, where there is another fine church. The coast is reached again at St. Mary's and the road has the company of the tiny "Romney, Hythe and Dymchurch Railway", a fascinating little line which is very popular with visitors. Rye to Hythe by this route, 25 miles.

From Hythe the route keeps along the coast by Sandgate, turning farther inland beyond this westerly suburb of Folkestone by the upper Sandgate road and then past the head post office to the Town Hall.

Folkestone (192) is both a busy port for the Continent and a popular resort. Besides these, it is an ancient town. From the east cliff the old town looks most attractive. The red-roofed fishing cottages will remind the tourist of Cornish villages. North-east of

Folkestone lies The Warren, a wild area of tumbled chalk between the cliffs and the shore. Fashionable Folkestone resorts to The Leas, a series of level lawns on the cliffs to the west of the harbour.

The Dover road mounts in great curves out of Folkestone and then traverses dull upland before dropping (care needed) into Dover.

Dover (199) is a busy port and resort and has now additional importance as the nearest large town to the Kent coalfield to the north. The town was subjected to heavy bombardments from France and from the air during the 1939-45 war, during which many civilians were evacuated to places of greater safety. The town and harbour lie in a hollow at the mouth of the River Dour. On the cliffs on both sides are fortifications and gun-sites. The side streets of Dover are steep and its narrow main arteries are often congested. Dover is a town with a character. The straits here are only 17 miles wide, and the town is the closest to the Continent of any in Britain. Dover was the starting point of the Roman road (or series of roads) known as Watling Street. It was a Norman stronghold and was often raided by the French. The castle (which should be visited) crowns a summit to the east of the town and the octagonal Roman pharos, or lighthouse, is perhaps the oldest standing building in Britain. Shakespeare Cliff, to the west, is so called from traditional association with the well-known passage in *King Lear*. The site of the English outlet to the often-proposed Channel Tunnel lies west of Shakespeare Cliff and exploratory shafts and other works are visible.

Dover has a youth hostel at 26 Eastcliff, and there are other places catering for cyclists. A stay of one or more nights is recommended at Dover.

A walking excursion from Dover lies along the cliff edge past the South Foreland, through the sheltered little resort of St. Margaret's Bay, past the Dover Patrol Memorial (1914-18) and along the Kingsdown Cliffs to Kingsdown; then along a made road by Walmer Castle, official residence of the Warden of the Cinque Ports (at present, 1949, Mr. Winston Churchill) and so into Deal. There is a good railway service back to Dover. Walking distance, about 10 miles.

North-west of Dover stretches a hilly countryside of great charm. Its topographical high spot is the Elham Valley, a deep trench between the downs. A splendid scenic round from Dover is through Siberts wold, Barham, Elham, Lyminge, Etchinghill, Paddlesworth and so into Dover again. Distance, about 10 miles.

The main road between Dover and Deal is not noteworthy and it is possible at Ringwould to turn right and reach the coast again at Kingsdown, passing Walmer Castle on the left before reaching Deal.

Deal (208) consists, once again, of an old village (inland) and a modern visitors' quarter close to the steep beach. Hereabouts is the reputed site of Julius Caesar's landing in 55 B.C. Off Deal lie the notorious Goodwin Sands, a series of sandbanks exposed at low water.

The main road from Upper Deal to Sandwich keeps well inland through low-lying country. An alternative, of approximately the same distance, keeps closer to the shore, passing the ruined Sandown Castle and then going over the golf links and eventually running into Sandwich from the east.

Sandwich (253) is a quaint place with old houses and twisting streets. It retains its ancient gates and has several old churches. About 1½ miles north-west from Sandwich, along a minor road, is **Richborough Castle**, where there are extensive Roman remains which are now cared for by H.M. Office of Works. Richborough stood at the mouth of the River Stour in a strong position. It was used as a supply base in the 1914-18 war.

Sandwich was one of the original Cinque Ports—the others were Dover, Hythe, Romney and Hastings. Rye and Winchelsea were added as "ancient towns", and other ports also adhered to the alliance, which in return for privileges had, on demand, to furnish ships for the royal fleet.

North of Sandwich are the resorts of the Isle of Thanet (see page 136). The main route does not enter these, however, but strikes westward for Canterbury, the principal attraction for tourists in East Kent, crossing the northern part of the Kent coalfield.

There is not a great deal to see along the Sandwich-Canterbury road, although the modern colleries and new villages add a certain

The Barbican
SANDWICH

interest. The road is an easy one, passing through Ash (where there is a notable church), Wingham and Littlebourne. On the descent into Canterbury from the hospital 1½ miles out there is a good view of the cathedral and the town around it.

Canterbury (221), the earliest city in the kingdom and the cradle of English Christianity, lies in a peaceful district of water and meadowland, with hop gardens also to give the scene an authentic touch of Kent. Entering along the Sandwich road, the cathedral is quickly approached. It lies to the right hand.

Canterbury was a Roman city and its main avenue is still represented by the east-west route along Watling Street. A burnt-down church and monastery were rebuilt in 1077 and in 1170 the murder of Thomas Becket, the archbishop, led to his canonisation as St. Thomas. During the next three centuries there were many pilgrimages to the shrine. The cathedral can usually be visited during daytime. It contains many monuments and the Bell Harry Tower (235 ft.) is a splendid example of its kind.

East of the cathedral (also seen on the entry by the Sandwich road) is St. Augustine's College, which occupies the site of a Benedictine monastery. Christ Church Gate, to the west of the cathedral, has been restored, but remains as a good piece of Perpendicular work. St. Martin's Church (again north of the Sandwich entrance to Canterbury) dates back to A.D. 597

Canterbury is recommended as a halting place for one night or more. There is a youth hostel in a rural situation two miles northward, on the Tyler Hill road. Other accommodation is available in the city and around.

The road between Canterbury and Rochester is described in reverse on pages 107–108, together with alternatives.

———————

South-east of Sittingbourne and 18 miles from Canterbury by Faversham, lies the hostel at **Doddington** in typical Kent country. It forms a base for an exploration of the Kentish part of the North Downs.

———————

The main road westward leads by Faversham, Sittingbourne, Rainham and Chatham to **Rochester** (248).

Over the bridge and right through Strood and the tourist is well on the way by **Gad's Hill**, the house where Dickens died (see page 107) and Chalk, into the modern industrial centre of **Gravesend** (256), where the tour nominally ends. There is a frequent service of trains back to London, while for those wishing to return by road the route is by Northfleet and along the by-passes to the south of Dartford and Welling as described on page 107. The northerner making for home can cross the Gravesend-Tilbury ferry and thus leave London well to the west.

———————

The tourist who does not mind missing Canterbury and wishes to follow the coastline closely round the Isle of Thanet and into the country to the west can do so readily from Sandwich. The countryside is not so attractive as other parts of Kent and Surrey, but it has quiet corners in spite of the popular and busy resorts in its earlier section.

From Sandwich the road first runs northward alongside Pegwell

Bay, passing the supposed landing place of the Saxons and Jutes under Hengist and Horsa.

Ramsgate is a port and resort in a sheltered dip between the chalk. Its southerly aspect is a pleasing feature. The place played a notable part in the reception of soldiers evacuated from Dunkirk in 1940—like all the coast towns between Margate and Dover. The "Golden Eagle" steamers ply from here (and from Margate) to London Bridge and carry cyclists and bicycles.

Broadstairs, three miles northward, is quieter and was a favourite of Dickens.

From Broadstairs the coast road keeps close to the cliff and passes North Foreland, before turning eastward and then northward again for Margate.

Margate is larger than Ramsgate and is a popular resort, a Blackpool of Kent, without any inhibitions. Wherever the wind comes from, Margate has a sea breeze. The newer part of the town is to the east and is called Cliftonville.

The eastward way keeps inland, passing the resorts of Westgate-on-Sea and Birchington-on-Sea. At Sarre a road comes in from Ramsgate, and two miles ahead the road going northward by Chislet for Reculver and Herne Bay is the one to follow.

Reculver, on the site of a Roman fort, is a seaside village with twin towers called the Sister Towers which act as a landmark. The coast hereabout is low-lying but not unattractive.

Herne Bay is a large resort with a smart esplanade. To the west, reached by a continuing series of lanes, is **Whitstable**, an old place joined to the modern resort of Tankerton to the east, and formerly the port of Canterbury and noted for its oysters.

A marshland road leads by Graveney and so into Faversham, on the Canterbury-Rochester road.

———————

The main tour of 256 miles from Portsmouth to Gravesend has halts at Arundel (two nights), Steyning, Eastbourne (or near), Rye, Dover (two nights) and Canterbury, making an eight-day tour in all. This could be shortened or lengthened as desired, by a higher daily mileage or by staying more than one night at several of the halts instead of at two. The tour described makes an excellent out-of-season holiday (say in April, May, October or November) because the halting places are often busy enough in season and only too glad of business out of it.

DAY AND WEEK-END RUNS INTO KENT

This series of guides aims, primarily, to direct the tourist rather than the day rider or the week-ender. There are, however, in Kent a number of distinctive attractions which are not, for geographical reasons, included in the main tour.

Typical of these destinations for day or week-end runs is **Kit's Coty House**, about five miles south of Rochester on the descent towards Maidstone from Bluebell Hill. The "House" is a dolmen, formed of three upright stones eight feet high, with a capstone 11 ft. long, supposedly the tomb of a British chief.

The youth hostel at **Kemsing**, a fine house in a quiet village on the Pilgrims' Way, lies about four miles north-east of Sevenoaks and makes a useful base for one of the best short rounds in Kent. South-east of Kemsing is **Ightham Mote**, an old manor house in wooded surroundings. From it pleasant lanes run south-west by Shipbourne and Leigh to **Penshurst Place**, just north of the village of Penshurst. The "Place" is another grand old mansion, with a fine fourteenth-century hall.

By going west from Penshurst and then north, the village of Chiddingstone can be reached. **Chiddingstone** is a charming place, with old timbered houses, a modern castle and the "Chiding Stone", reputed to be a judgment seat.

From Chiddingstone lanes strike north-west to Crockham Hill in a well-wooded range which drops to the north into the old-fashioned small town of **Westerham**. From Westerham there is a comparatively little-used by-road route back to Croydon and London by Westerham Hill, Biggin Hill and Addington.

Cycling on the South Coast today

As Harold Briercliffe wrote this cycle route guide in the late 1940s, many of the roads he mentions are now busier than they were and are not suitable for cycling today. Suggested alternative cycle routes, from Sustrans, which are in the same location as Harold's original route are listed below. To devise your own detailed route and map in the region, go to www.sustrans.org.uk/map for online mapping, and free iphone and android cycling apps.

National Route 2 runs almost the entire length of the south coast of England (with a few short gaps still to be filled). You can follow over 110 miles of unbroken National Route 2 from **Littlehampton East** to **Dover.** This stretch takes in some wonderful seafront promenades and interesting towns with Brighton and Hove being excellent places to stop.

The National Cycle Network's longest route, **National Route 1**, begins in **Dover** and winds roughly round the coastline taking in **Deal, Sandwich, Canterbury, Gravesend** and **Dartford** before entering the east side of London. Between Dover and Dartford, National Route 1 is roughly 85 miles of road and traffic-free cycle routes. There is a lovely stretch of this route between St Margarets at **Cliffe** and **Deal**, which is partly on seaside promenades and leads you to Deal Castle with many wonderful views on route.

National Route 18 is largely an on-road route that runs from **Canterbury** eastwards to **Royal Tunbridge Wells**, which is roughly 60 miles. This route is an excellent way to take in Kent's quintessential garden of England scenery, complete with hops, apple orchards, oast houses and picture-postcard villages. However, anybody who thinks Kent is flat might reconsider after this ride, which is not recommended for novice riders.

Useful maps and books (available from www.sustransshop.co.uk): *Kent and East Sussex Cycle Tours; Kent: Cycling Country Lanes (Goldeneye Cycling Map); Explore Kent by Bike.*

ORGANIZATIONS AND MAPS

Sustrans Cycle Mapping

View 25,000 miles of cycle routes, including 13,000 miles of National Cycle Network online using Sustrans interactive mapping. Visit: **www.sustrans.org.uk/map**

You can also:
- Draw your routes, measure distances and share your favourite journey with others.
- Find local amenities including bike shops / hire centres, shops, schools and local attractions.

See every bus stop and train station in the UK with links to their timetables.

The Complete National Cycle Network App

Access our online mapping from your pocket with the Complete National Cycle Network app. The app includes all of our online features as well as:
- GPS tracking – record your route and share it with friends
- Store the map backgrounds for an area when you have no mobile signal

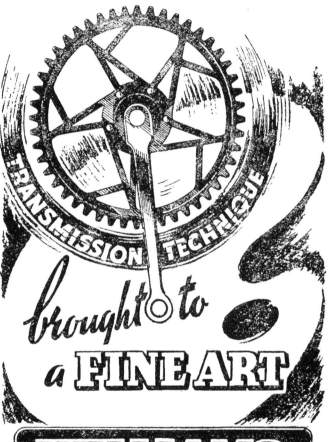

TRANSMISSION TECHNIQUE

brought to

a FINE ART

WILLIAMS
CHAIN WHEELS & CRANKS

144

CHOOSE *Your* CYCLE FROM
BRITAIN'S FINEST RANGE

In the products of Raleigh Industries Limited you have a choice of bicycles which represent the very latest developments in cycle manufacture anywhere in the world, and in Robin Hood, a bicycle of remarkable quality for so low a price. On any one of these machines you are assured of trouble-free cycling for years to come.

Outstanding features of
Raleigh, Rudge and Humber:
● DYNOLUXE EQUIPMENT giving car-type lighting ● BUILT IN THIEF-PROOF LOCK ● STAINLESS STEEL SPOKES ● RUST-PROOFED ENAMEL FINISH ● HANDLEBAR "FLICK" TRIGGER CONTROL to Sturmey-Archer 3 or 4 Speed Gear.

RALEIGH
THE ALL-STEEL BICYCLE

RUDGE
Britain's Best Bicycle

HUMBER
The Aristocrat of Bicycles

'Easy on the Road - Light on the Purse'

M.8.

145

INDEX